GALATOIRE'S
COOKBOOK

By LEON GALATOIRE

PELICAN PUBLISHING COMPANY
Gretna 1998

First printing, 1994
Second printing, 1998

The word "Pelican" and the depiction of a pelican are trademarks
of Pelican Publishing Company, Inc.,
and are registered in the U.S. Patent and Trademark Office.

Library of Congress Cataloging-in-Publication Data

Galatoire, Leon.
    Galatoire's cookbook / Leon Galatoire.
       p. cm.
    Includes index.
    ISBN 0-88289-999-6
    1. Cookery, American—Louisiana style. 2. Galatoire's Restaurant.
I. Title. II. Title: Cookbook.
TX715.2.L68G35 1994
641.5'09763'35—dc20   93-37308
                                          CIP

Manufactured in the United States of America

Published by Pelican Publishing Company, Inc.
P.O. Box 3110, Gretna, Louisiana 70054-3110

To my loving mother, Leonie Evans Galatoire,
whose support over the years has helped me attain
some very special goals,
and this project is the culmination
of her support and love

Great food is only for those who take the time to enjoy it.

LEON GALATOIRE

Contents

Acknowledgments

I wish to express my gratitude to my dear friends, Roy and Mimi Guste, whose efforts were truly instrumental in the conception and completion of this project.

Special thanks to my entire family, past and present, who have worked hard individually and collectively to build Galatoire's Restaurant into the great institution that it is—Jean Galatoire, Justin Galatoire, Leon Galatoire, Gabriel Galatoire, Rene Galatoire, Gabe Galatoire, Yvonne Galatoire Wynne, Doug Wynne, Chris Ansel, Sr., Chris Ansel, Jr., David Gooch, and Justin Galatoire Frey.

And special thanks to George Dureau, whose brilliant artwork blesses my book cover.

And I wish to acknowledge the people at Pelican Publishing Company for recognizing my work for what it is.

Introduction

The Development of Creole Cuisine

In 1718, when Bienville broke ground on this spot that we now call New Orleans, he also began the pot simmering on the development of New Orleans Creole cuisine.

That very day of his ground-breaking, the Indian guides in his party built the cooking fires and supplied the vegetables, fish, game, and seasoning herbs that were put into the pot to make the very first Creole meal. Who of that party of some fifty men would have understood that that very pot of food, that first meal in New Orleans was the seed that would grow into America's most important, most expansive, indigenous cuisine? However, all things considered, even had a full understanding of our present-day cooking we call Creole been conceived, it is hard to imagine that things could have developed better culinarily then they have.

To understand the recipes that I have set forth here—classic New Orleans Creole recipes, personal renditions of family recipes, and an assortment of my own creations—it is necessary to understand the development of New Orleans cuisine itself.

The meager beginnings of Creole cooking came from the first infusion of Louisiana Indian cookery into simple country French cooking, or vice versa, depending on your historical viewpoint. The French may have been adept at cooking in their own country or in Canada from where Bienville had recently come, but they were hardly prepared to make the best use of the abundance of indigenous, still peculiar, Louisiana products. When the Indians offered their help, the French promptly and necessarily accepted.

So, the beginning of Creole cuisine is the combination of French and Louisiana Indian. By the time that 1718 stew had simmered over the years, by 1762 it was well advanced as a cuisine employing most all available local products.

In 1762, the French crown transferred the ownership of Louisiana and New Orleans to the Spanish and the envoys of the Spanish crown arrived to take hold of the steerage of the colony.

Easy riches were what the French, then the Spanish, were after. It was gold, silver, and copper mines and pearl fisheries that were being searched for. When these treasures were not found, the French, then the Spanish, failed to realize in the early stages of the development of the colony that the treasure that *was* so readily available to them for their plucking was the food products of the Americas that they had not yet recognized for the great value they were to become to the entire world.

France and Spain utilized these New World products such as corn, peppers, tomatoes, beans, squash, and potatoes in the further development of the cuisine of their own countries, but made them a far more important base of the cuisine developing in Louisiana itself. In Europe, the French and the Spanish had begun cultivating these New World vegetables as early as the beginning of the sixteenth century, so that by the time our forefathers arrived in New Orleans, they were already familiar, to a degree, with the culinary possibilities of these foods.

It was the Spanish that became the third important influence in Creole cuisine, after Louisiana Indian and French. It was during the period of Spanish domination that Creole cooking began resembling the Creole cuisine that we know and enjoy today.

Another important influence in the development of Creole cuisine is that of the Africans who came here first as slaves to work the sugarcane plantations of the French. They brought with them their own foods such as the yam and okra, but even more importantly, theirs were the hands that worked magic in the pot for the settlers and colonists. It was their cooking abilities that brought all these influences together to consummate the marriage of French, Indian, and Spanish from which issued their New World progeny, Creole cuisine.

When New Orleans and Louisiana was returned to France from the Spanish in 1803, and immediately transferred to the ownership of the United States, the city began to grow in a hurried fashion that was until then unknown in this thriving, Europeanlike city. Hotels and boarding houses sprung up in great profusion in answer to the new growth in business and port activity, resulting in growing business and residency.

The original plan for New Orleans was drawn up by Le Blond De La Tour, with the specific instruction to name important streets after the French royalty and their patron saints. The rues d'Orleans and Bourbon—Galatoire's Restaurant is located on Bourbon Street—were named after members of the Bourbon royal family, and the city was named after Philippe II, Duc d'Orleans, Regent of France, and brother of the recently deceased Louis XIV.

In 1715, Louis XV was not quite ready to take the throne at his great-grandfather's death: he was only five years old. Until he reached the age of thirteen—his legal majority—his uncle, Philippe, Duc d'Orleans, acted as regent.

After many disasters—famine, hurricanes, and fire—Bourbon Street was built into one of the city's most fashionable streets, the site of many strong, sturdy mansions of the city's elite. It was on this street that Galatoire's was to emerge as New Orleans' most cherished restaurant.

A Brief History of Galatoire's Restaurant

It was my great-uncle, Jean Galatoire, who was the man responsible for beginning his unpretentious cafe on Bourbon Street that has become New Orleans' most cherished restaurant.

Jean Galatoire was born in Pau, France, to a family of innkeepers. But as the family business was a humble one, he struck out on his own to make his fortune in America. He settled first in Birmingham, Alabama, where he owned a small inn and restaurant. From Birmingham, in the early 1890s, Jean made his way to Chicago, to the world's fair, this country's greatest exposition, where he tried his hand—apparently with much success—at the cafe business, finding it very much to his liking. With his earnings from Chicago, he gambled on New Orleans as the right place to try his hand again in the cafe business in a more permanent fashion.

When Jean arrived in New Orleans, he was quick to study the existing restaurants, making friends with their owners, learning what he could from them about New Orleans and its unique Creole cuisine. He opened a small cafe on Dauphine Street, while setting his sights on the ambitious quest of purchasing one of the city's well-respected existing establishments, Victor's Restaurant on Bourbon Street. He ingratiated himself to the aging Monsieur Victor Bero, who took so kindly to Jean that before he retired, Victor agreed to sell his restaurant to Galatoire. But even before

Victor had handed over the restaurant to Galatoire, the two had become inseparable friends, so much so, and so often was Galatoire to be found together with Bero in the dining room, that some New Orleanians actually began calling it Galatoire's Restaurant. Monsieur Victor was at first annoyed at this but soon relaxed into the comfort of the sale that would bring an easy and successful transition of his life's work into the hands of a capable operator. In 1905, Victor's officially became Galatoire's, and Jean set to work even harder to bring the people of New Orleans to his dining room.

Just as Antoine Alciatore of Antoine's Restaurant and Elizabeth Kettering Begue of Madame Begue's had earned their reputations by serving the cognoscenti of the city and well-heeled travelers, so did Jean Galatoire earn a reputation for laying out one of the finest tables in New Orleans. The wealthy and influential cotton merchants and the proprietors of Canal Street's leading department stores and shops soon made Galatoire's their home for both themselves and for their visiting friends and clientele.

Jean's success required the assistance of others in the management of the restaurant. He invited his nephews in Pau, France—Justin, Gabriel, and Leon—to come to New Orleans to work with him. They did come and eventually purchased Galatoire's from their Uncle Jean in 1916, at which time he retired.

The next active generation of operators involved in the restaurant came with one of Justin's four daughters, Yvonne, followed by two of Leon's sons, Rene and my father Gabe. Gabriel, my father's uncle, had no children and continued quite a colorful tenure at Galatoire's until his death in the mid-1940s.

Currently, the fourth-generation owners and operators are David Gooch, grandson of Leon; Justin Frey, grandson of Justin; and myself.

My Own Remembrances

My memories of growing up here, and my lifelong affair with food and Galatoire's Restaurant, are my most cherished possessions. Let me share a glimpse with you.

One long-ago evening, when I was very young, I recall my mother driving us down Canal Street in New Orleans, on the way to

Galatoire's, to bring my father to work. I was in the backseat with my face pinned to the window. As we turned off Canal onto Bourbon Street and drove the one block to the restaurant where we stopped to let my father off, I remember being amazed at the number of people standing in line in front waiting to get into where he worked. I made the connection for the first time that this was the place we would come to visit him in the daytime, where the goings-on in the kitchen particularly fascinated me. The delicious smells of the simmering sauces, roasting birds, and grilling meats were as exciting as the action of the cooks, deftly wielding their pots, whisks, and knives. That was when I first began anticipating the time when I might be able to be a part of this excitement myself.

When we would leave the restaurant after visiting my father, my mother would drive us down Bourbon Street on our way back home. We'd pass all the burlesque and strip joints, the jazz clubs, Al Hirt's, and Pete Fountain's. Loud barkers were out front at every door, swinging the doors quickly open to every passerby for a quick glimpse of the entertainment inside. It was a first revelation in my life. I knew then that someday I wanted to be part of Galatoire's Restaurant on Bourbon Street in New Orleans.

It was a year or so later, though, that I had my next food revelation. My Uncle Buddy, my mother's brother, had a fishing camp at Empire, a fishing village near the mouth of the Mississippi where it flows into the Gulf of Mexico. We would go down there to stay with Uncle Buddy who loved love to cook for his guests and fellow fishermen. Uncle Buddy liked the cooking part more than my father did. Although he was not associated with the restaurant business, he had acquired a great love for cooking, a love that he imparted to me from early on.

Friday afternoons we would leave New Orleans, begin the hour-and-a-half drive, and head down to the camp where we stayed the entire weekend through to Sunday afternoon. The camp itself was a large rustic place built on pilings, about twelve feet above the water, allowing for high water from storms and dreaded hurricanes. The place was simple—disposable in a way—but well set up for fishing, cooking, and entertaining. Uncle Buddy had built the camp with a few friends; there was enough space to sleep fifteen people. In those days, cooking and entertaining at the camp was equal to, if not more important than, the fishing itself.

Friday night would begin with Buddy sitting me down in the camp's kitchen (I was only six or seven years old), or outside on the pier over the water, with a large hamper of freshly caught shrimp—that day's prize from an afternoon's trawl. There I would sit either alone, or with other cousins, and do my appointed job of peeling the shrimp. Sitting on the pier I would throw the shells in the water, and the shrimp into a pot to bring inside. The discarded shells in the water would attract fish that would churn up the water below me as they nibbled on the shells. On some occasions an intrepid raccoon, observing the action, would swim out from the land to feed on the fish, or any shrimp I might let drop his way. Sometimes that basket of shrimp was so big and full that to save time I would let a few drop into the raccoon's paws. It pleased both of us.

With the all the shrimp peeled (or fed to the fish and raccoon), I would return to the kitchen where the men would be gathered, having a few beers, telling each other the same fish tales that they told every time they went to the camp for the weekend. A gumbo would already be simmering on the stove. The shrimp didn't go in until the last so I would join in, have a root beer or red drink, and listen to the stories again. Then we would all sit down to a grand meal.

The morning would begin early at 4 A.M. when breakfast would be started: a spread of eggs, homemade biscuits, Creole sausages, and sweet, Louisiana strawberry jam. With all this behind us it was time for the event. We would all climb into the boat—an old wooden cabin cruiser converted for fishing—and head off to the fishing areas out through Southwest Pass, leading into the Gulf. There we would tie up to the oil rigs where the smaller fish schooled to feed on barnacles on the underwater structure of the oil rigs, and larger fish would feed on them. By 7 A.M. we were fishing. We caught red snapper, trout, cobia (lemon fish), and many varieties that were less desirable and would be returned to the waters. No matter how rough the waters were, if the fish were biting, we stayed to fish. Sometimes they would have to put me off the boat onto the still platform of the drilling rig so I could recover awhile from the queasiness caused from the rocking and rolling of the boat in the

Gulf waves. The day would pass and the iceboxes would fill.

On our return to the camp we would clean the boat, clean the fish, and then cook lunch, which was usually gumbo from the day before.

The dinner, the whole process of cooking the evening's meal, would begin again. Usually we would boil the crabs and fry and sauté the fish caught earlier in the day. It was always a big production with each individual contributing some entry to the meal's entire menu. Rough as it was at the camp, the meals were as fine as can be had anywhere in Louisiana. The process of beginning the fishing trip, trawling for shrimp, crabbing, making the gumbo, boiling the seafood, and frying the fish, all being finally brought to the table in its final execution, was the total experience that began to develop in me a beginning interest in the restaurant business, my father's restaurant.

During high school, I spent those years at a school on the Gulf Coast, not far from New Orleans, where we were able, being on the Gulf, to fish and enjoy the water and its varieties of seafood. Even the food served in the cafeteria had a memorable difference from what I saw served in other friends' schools' cafeterias, in that there were always fresh seafood and good cooks who knew how to prepare delicious Southern meals.

When high school was over, I left for Europe to travel for a summer before college, while experiencing firsthand the excitingly varied cuisines there.

I spent some time in France where I was particularly impressed with the undivided affinity the French had for their food. I also observed the tremendous respect they had for their cuisine, not only in its preparation, but where it came from and what it took to get it. I can well remember thinking that these people are very serious about their culinary arts.

I know that travel in itself is an invaluable source of education. Over the years I have had the good fortune of being able to afford to travel extensively abroad as well as to many other places of interest. This travel has allowed me to reach a higher level of expertise in my field.

Some of these places, such as Spain, France, Mexico, and most of the islands in the West Indies, have a direct influence on New Orleans and our particular style of cooking. One of the things I would like to project in this book is a taste of these different ethnic flavors through some recipes I have developed as a result of my travels, as well as keeping some at home with our own more traditional examples. I also experimented with some interesting variations on classic dishes.

In college in New Orleans at Loyola University, I attended night school and worked in restaurants as a waiter and apprentice cook to test for any talent I might have for the business itself. Although I already had developed a great interest in food and cooking, I wanted to learn and experience other aspects of the restaurant business before I actually made any decision to devote myself to it, and to approach my own family about employment at Galatoire's.

These apprentice jobs brought me to Houston, and then a return to New Orleans where I became more interested in management in the restaurant business. It was then that I had to make my decision on joining the family in the operation of Galatoire's. After some serious thought, I did decide to join my family at the restaurant, and have ever since been proud of the association, and that decision.

Once entrenched in Galatoire's, I began a four-year tenure as cook, wherein I learned the superb repertoire of dishes that make up the Galatoire's menu. During those four years, when I would have an opportunity for some brief time off, I usually headed down to the Caribbean, a place that drew me; I loved the cultures of the islands, and the food of the people. The Caribbean will always influence the way I think about food.

At Galatoire's I learned the fundamentals of its particular kitchen operation, from chopping onions to peeling potatoes to the larger direction of sauces and important dishes. The other necessary fundamentals of the operation of a kitchen and its management was also an important part of that four-year tenure.

One thing that impressed me in particular was the lack of modern appliances, and that all of the sauces were made by hand, each ingredient hand-chopped, even in the large many-gallon quantities that we prepared. It was good to work side by side with the older cooks who had been there for many years: they had a great deal to teach me.

On my first day—I was twenty-two then—I washed and chopped vegetables. From there I learned techniques and processes, moving from station to station on the prep and cooking "line," until I knew the proper way to perform each step in the cooking process. I worked every position on the line, a curriculum of my own design. From the sauté station I moved to the fry station, and on to the sauce station, which is the backbone of the food at Galatoire's as well as most restaurants.

The bulk of the work occurred in the early morning before the doors were open. It was then the food was prepped for final cooking at service times.

I was in the kitchen for four years, and then moved into the dining room as manager, while continuing to experiment with new dishes of my own invention.

Now that I have returned to the kitchen to head the staff in the preparation of all food served at Galatoire's, I have more opportunity to experiment and explore new recipes and directions for the contemporary audience.

This book is a collection of time-tested traditional New Orleans recipes, as well as a grouping of new recipes of my own design.

Galatoire's is a restaurant to be proud of, a truly New Orleans restaurant. Just as in Jean's day, everyone still waits in line to be seated—no reservations are accepted—and no degree of celebrity will alter that rule. The clientele at lunchtime is a veritable Who's Who of the local social and business worlds. Even today, the critics who really know New Orleans restaurants, the locals, choose Galatoire's as the quintessential New Orleans restaurant.

This book, an endeavor that has long been growing in me as a necessity, is now a reality of which I am exceedingly proud. Enjoy these recipes as I do. They are what I have to contribute to New Orleans' grand culinary legacy.

Appetizers

ANCHOVY CANAPE

Nothing could be more appealing to the lover of the anchovy and no dish could be more simple. In years past, the import business in New Orleans brought goods from all over the world that were often unheard of elsewhere in this country. Anchovies were considered a delicacy, especially with the Italian community here who had their own shops and market stalls that dealt exclusively with imported Italian products.

6 slices toast
3 dozen anchovy filets
6 lettuce leaves

3 hard-boiled eggs, finely
  chopped

Cover each slice of toast with 6 anchovy filets. Trim the crusts from the toast with a sharp knife. Cut each slice of toast into four pieces. Garnish each plate with a lettuce leaf filled with some of the chopped hard-boiled egg. *Serves 6.*

CRABMEAT COCKTAIL

This appetizer is called a cocktail because it is served in a cocktail glass. It is also interesting to note that the word *cocktail* was coined in New Orleans.

This cold, ketchup-based sauce is one that is used with all boiled and fried seafoods, as well as with raw oysters on the half-shell. It can be made and kept tightly covered for two weeks in the refrigerator.

1 cup cocktail sauce
1 lb. jumbo lump crabmeat

1 lemon, cut into wedges

Arrange four 4-ounce chilled or frosted cocktail glasses with 4 oz. of crabmeat in each. Top with 2 oz. of cocktail sauce and serve cold with lemon wedges. *Serves 4.*

SPLIT ARTICHOKE
WITH GARLIC CREAM

The artichoke is another product that arrived with the Spanish during their possession of Louisiana. It remains a popular vegetable, cooked in more ways here than in most other cuisines of the world, having even become part of the traditional meal served on the Catholic-observed Good Friday.

4 large artichokes	2 cloves minced garlic
1 tbsp. vinegar	⅓ cup olive oil
Enough cold water to cover artichokes	Salt to taste
	Pepper to taste
7 qt. water, salted	½ tsp. lemon juice
2 tbsp. Dijon mustard	2 tsp. finely chopped parsley

Trim the tip ends of the leaves from artichokes using a pair of scissors. Add vinegar to the cold water and then soak the artichokes. Soaking in the vinegar will prevent discoloration.

In a large pot, bring the salted water to a rolling boil. Drop in the artichokes and allow to boil for 35-40 minutes, or until a leaf pulled from the choke proves tender.

During this time, prepare the mustard sauce as follows. In a medium mixing bowl, combine mustard and garlic. Using a wire whisk, slowly incorporate olive oil at a dribble, constantly whipping until sauce becomes thick and creamy. Season with salt and pepper. Add lemon juice and refrigerate.

Drain the artichokes in a colander and, when cool enough to handle, split into lengthwise slices with a serrated knife. Remove and discard chokes.

Serve cold, with the mustard sauce—garnished with the chopped parsley—in a side dish for dipping. *Serves 8.*

CELERY RIBS STUFFED WITH ASPARAGUS AND BLUE CHEESE

Simple as this may seem, hot summer meals in New Orleans often call for simple fare and cool tasty tidbits to compliment cocktails before dinner.

The crispness of the celery, the tastiness of the asparagus, and the smooth saltiness of the blue cheese meld well together for this purpose.

16 asparagus
Enough salted water to cover
   asparagus tips
1 head celery (approximately 8
   ribs)
1 small yellow onion, minced
1 cup crumbled blue cheese
Salt to taste
¼ tsp. white pepper, or to taste
½ cup whipping cream

In a medium pot, blanch the asparagus tips in enough salted water to cover for 3 minutes.

Trim the celery ribs under cold water, slice each rib in half crosswise.

In a medium mixing bowl, combine minced onion, crumbled blue cheese, salt, pepper, and whipping cream. Fold mixture until thoroughly blended. Refrigerate mixture to chill for 30 minutes.

Trim the celery ribs and asparagus to equal lengths. Place one asparagus tip into each trimmed celery rib and top with the blue cheese mixture. Chill to serve. *Makes 16 pieces.*

Note: This recipe is also included as a salad.

GRILLED CHICKEN BREASTS BELIZE

I could not resist the temptation to develop a dish that incorporated Caribbean flavors into New Orleans Creole cooking. Creole mustard and Louisiana hot sauce, along with the spices of the Caribbean, finished with a lime wedge is a delightful marriage, I assure you.

¼ cup red wine vinegar
¼ cup Creole mustard
1 tbsp. allspice, ground
14 tsp. ground nutmeg
½ tsp. Louisiana hot sauce
Dash cayenne pepper

Dash black pepper
⅔ cup vegetable oil
4 boneless, skinless chicken
   breasts, halved
1 lime, cut into wedges

For the marinade, combine the vinegar, mustard, allspice, nutmeg, hot sauce, cayenne, and black pepper in a small mixing bowl. Using a wire whisk, slowly beat in the oil at a dribble, allowing the ingredients to emulsify.

Slice the chicken breasts diagonally into finger-sized pieces. Place the chicken pieces into the marinade and be sure to coat all sides. Cover with plastic wrap and refrigerate overnight.

Preheat the grill using hot embers. Grill the chicken pieces for approximately 2 minutes on each side or until cooked through. Garnish with lime wedges. *Serves 4-6.*

CRABMEAT CANAPE MAYONNAISE

Using some of our most cherished foods—Creole mustard, lump crabmeat, and French bread—I have developed this savory cold appetizer to be easily served and shared at cocktail parties, as well as at the dinner table.

Make enough. They disappear as soon as they are passed on trays or placed on the table.

½ tsp. lemon juice
1 level tbsp. Creole mustard
¾ cup mayonnaise
Salt to taste
Pinch cayenne pepper
Pinch white pepper

½ cup finely chopped green onions
1 tbsp. finely chopped parsley
1 lb. jumbo lump crabmeat
2 loaves French bread, cut into rounds and toasted

In a medium mixing bowl, combine the lemon juice, Creole mustard, mayonnaise, salt, peppers, green onions, and parsley. Using a wire whisk, mix well. Fold in the crabmeat until mixture is well blended, but still keeping the lump crabmeat intact. Refrigerate covered for 1 hour. Serve on toasted French bread rounds. *Makes 2 dozen pieces.*

CANAPE LORENZO

It's difficult to know who all the names of dishes once or still belong to. My memory of Lorenzo is that he was a neighborhood pharmacist who was friends with my grandfather Leon, and who frequented our restaurant during my grandfather's proprietorship. As friends will do, grandfather named this dish after his friend to "immortalize" him in New Orleans.

That may have well been the case because the name Lorenzo has appeared on a number of restaurant menus here, all owing, perhaps, to the friendship between the restaurateur and the pharmacist.

1 cup Béchamel sauce
Salt to taste
Pinch cayenne pepper
White pepper to taste
½ cup finely chopped green onions
3 tbsp. clarified butter (reserve 1 tbsp. for finish)

1 lb. jumbo lump crabmeat
2 egg yolks
1 tbsp. fine bread crumbs
1 tsp. grated Parmesan cheese
4 slices toast
1 tsp. finely chopped parsley
1 lemon, cut into wedges

Prepare the Béchamel sauce. Season with salt, cayenne pepper, and white pepper.

In a medium saucepan, sauté the green onions in 2 tbsp. of the clarified butter over medium heat until tender. Add the crabmeat then fold in the Béchamel sauce. When mixture begins to simmer, remove from the heat and fold in the egg yolks. Refrigerate for 10 minutes. The mixture will become firm so as to mold for canapés as it cools.

During this time, preheat the oven to 350 degrees. Combine the bread crumbs and Parmesan cheese in a mixing bowl and blend well. Trim four slices of toast into 4-inch rounds. Place the rounds on a cookie sheet then spoon equal amounts of the crabmeat mixture onto each round using an ice-cream scoop.

Sprinkle the canapés well with the bread crumb/cheese mixture. Dot each with an equal portion of the remaining tablespoon of clarified butter then place into the oven to bake for 20 minutes. Transfer to serving plates hot. Garnish with parsley and lemon wedges. *Serves 4.*

CRABMEAT MAISON

Although similar to Crabmeat Canapé Mayonnaise, this other dish includes capers, which change the flavor considerably.

The fact that it is served on a bed of romaine leaves makes this more of a salad than the other, and could be served even as a light entrée.

½ tsp. lemon juice
1 level tbsp. Creole mustard
¾ cup mayonnaise
Salt to taste
Pinch cayenne pepper
Pinch white pepper
½ cup finely chopped green
    onions

1 tbsp. capers
1 tbsp. finely chopped parsley
1 lb. jumbo lump crabmeat
1 head romaine (the heart and
    more tender leaves chopped)

In a medium mixing bowl, combine the lemon juice, Creole mustard, mayonnaise, salt, peppers, green onions, capers, and parsley. Using a wire whisk, mix well. Fold in the crabmeat until mixture is well blended, but still keeping the lump crabmeat intact. Refrigerate covered for 1 hour. Serve on a bed of chopped romaine leaves. *Serves 4.*

CRABMEAT REMOULADE

The etymology of the word *remoulade* is believed by some culinary historians to have derived from the French word from the Picardy province of Remoula. Although the word describes the black radish, and there are none in the New Orleans recipe, it may have been that the early French remoulades were a salad including the black radish, although more commonly employing celeriac.

Our remoulade is served with seafood and most often with shrimp. This crabmeat version is a particular favorite of well-heeled natives.

This dish is prepared precisely as is the Shrimp Remoulade, substituting 2 lbs. crabmeat for the shrimp. *Serves 8.*

ESCARGOT BORDELAISE

Bordelaise means in the fashion of Bordeaux, France, or the fashion of the Bordeaux wife and cook. It is in this region where many of the greatest wines of the world are produced. The vineyards are home to the escargot, or snail, that must be harvested daily to prevent them from feasting on the precious grape vines.

The New Orleans Creoles inherited much of their culinary ingenuity from their French ancestors. Turning the plague of snails into a *chef d'oeuvre* is typical of French sagacity.

2 dozen escargot
½ cup clarified butter
Salt to taste
⅛ tsp. black pepper
1 tbsp. minced garlic, mixed with 1 tbsp. vegetable oil
1 tbsp. chopped parsley
8 toasted French bread rounds

Rinse escargot in cold water, pat dry. Sauté in clarified butter for 3 minutes over a low heat setting. Season with salt and pepper, add garlic and oil mixture, and continue to sauté for an additional 2 minutes.

Using a slotted spoon, remove the snails from the butter sauce and transfer them to perforated escargot serving dishes.

Add the parsley to the butter sauce, then pour over the escargot. Serve with toasted bread rounds. *Serves 4.*

ESCARGOT ROCKEFELLER
AU CHARTREUSE

In the 1890s, Jules Alciatore, second-generation proprietor of Antoine's Restaurant, invented Oysters Rockefeller, and because of the recipe's richness, named it after America's wealthiest citizen—John D. Rockefeller.

The undying popularity of the oyster recipe encouraged me to invent a snail dish using my own version of the Rockefeller sauce.

36 canned escargot	**Pinch ground thyme**
1½ cups clarified butter	**Pinch ground anise**
3 cups chopped spinach	**Salt to taste**
½ cup finely chopped green onions	**¼ tsp. black pepper**
	⅓ tsp. white pepper
½ cup finely chopped yellow onions	**1 tbsp. red wine vinegar**
	2 tbsp. Worcestershire sauce
⅓ cup finely chopped parsley	**2 tbsp. green Chartreuse**
1 rib chopped celery	**1 tsp. herbsaint**
1 tbsp. minced garlic	**1 cup fine French bread crumbs**

Preheat oven to 400 degrees. Rinse escargot in cold water. Drain, then sauté in ½ cup of the clarified butter for 2 or 3 minutes until tender. Remove from heat then place escargot on a dry cloth or paper towel. Put aside.

To make the Rockefeller sauce, in a food processor combine the spinach, green onions, yellow onions, parsley, celery, garlic, thyme, anise, salt, black pepper, white pepper, red wine vinegar, Worcestershire, Chartreuse, herbsaint, and remaining clarified butter (1 cup).

Puree the above ingredients until well blended. Put the mixture into a mixing bowl and fold in the bread crumbs, blending well.

Arrange escargot in six individual perforated baking dishes or small, oven-safe casserole dishes. Fill a pastry bag with the Rockefeller sauce, then squeeze out a small amount covering each escargot (about a teaspoon). Place casseroles in preheated oven and bake for 15 minutes. Serve hot. *Serves 6.*

SAUTEED LEEKS BEARNAISE

The leek most probably found its way here with the Germans who came early to farm some of the early plantations for other French owners. It was soon after the arrival of the Germans that their industry proved superior to the other settlers and they were quickly able to acquire their own lands to farm.

Fortunately for the city of New Orleans, when famine and hurricanes came close to destroying the burgeoning colony, it was the Germans who supplied the much-needed vegetable staples to right their provision needs.

1 cup Béarnaise Sauce
8 ripe leeks
Enough water to cover leeks

1 tsp. salt, to add to the water
4 tbsp. clarified butter

Prepare Béarnaise Sauce and put aside.

Peel the outer skin layers from the leeks to the young and tender core. Trim off the green portion allowing only the white section for cooking. Rinse in cold water. Boil in salted water for 5 minutes. Remove leeks and drain excess water onto a dry cloth.

Place leeks into a large saucepan with the clarified butter and sauté lightly for an additional 5 minutes. Again, remove and drain excess butter onto a dry cloth.

Arrange leeks onto small serving plates, top with warm Béarnaise Sauce, and serve. *Serves 4.*

OYSTERS BIENVILLE

Oysters Bienville have long been related to the restaurant Arnaud but they were actually an invention of Roy Louis Alciatore, third-generation proprietor of Antoine's Restaurant, and his chef of many years, Auguste ("Pete") Michel.

The dish was concocted for a special gourmet dinner at which Arnaud Cazenave, owner of Arnaud's Restaurant, was in attendance. Cazenave loved the dish so much that he coaxed the recipe out of Alciatore and claimed it as his own.

3 dozen oysters on the half-
  shell
6 cups rock salt
4 oz. bacon
½ cup finely chopped shallots
½ cup clarified butter
2 tbsp. flour
½ cup half & half cream,
  heated

1 lb. shrimp, ground
1 cup finely chopped
  mushrooms
2 oz. white wine
3 egg yolks
1 tsp. parsley, finely chopped
⅓ cup fine bread crumbs
  combined with ¼ cup
  Parmesan cheese

Preheat oven to 400 degrees. Arrange oysters in shells in six pie pans half-filled with rock salt. Place in the oven for 10 minutes until the edges curl. Remove and set aside.

Cut bacon strips into small pieces and fry until brown. Put aside.

In a medium saucepan, sauté the shallots in clarified butter until tender. Add flour and whisk until smooth. Gradually pour in the hot half & half cream while whisking constantly until the sauce thickens. Add bacon, shrimp, mushrooms, and white wine. Allow to simmer for 10 minutes over a low heat setting, stirring constantly.

Remove from heat and add egg yolks and parsley. Blend well. Allow sauce to set for 10-15 minutes.

Spoon sauce carefully over each oyster in its shell, then sprinkle each generously with the bread crumb/Parmesan mixture. Bake at 400 degrees until tops brown, approximately 5 minutes. Serve very hot. *Serves 6.*

OYSTERS EN BROCHETTE

This is a delightful dish that is perfect for those jaded palates that yearn for full, rich flavors—no subtlety here. The bacon complements the oysters' flavor superbly.

It is interesting to me that many of my friends who are chefs and restaurateurs order this dish as often as any other dish on our menu at Galatoire's.

18 strips of bacon	Dash Tabasco sauce
36 large oysters	2 cups cooking oil
2 cups milk	2 cups flour
1 egg	3 slices toast, cut in wedges
Pinch of salt	6 lemon wedges
⅛ tsp. white pepper	1 tbsp. finely chopped parsley

Cut each bacon strip in half. Blanch bacon in boiling water for 3 minutes. Remove and place on paper towel and pat dry.

Arrange oysters and bacon strips on brochette skewers, alternating one oyster then one bacon strip, etc., with a half-dozen on each skewer.

In a medium mixing bowl, combine the milk, egg, salt, pepper, and Tabasco to make a batter and whisk well. Preheat oil in a deep frying pan over a medium heat setting. Pour flour into a baking pan with 2-inch sides. Dip the brochettes into the batter to fully cover then dredge into flour. Shake off excess flour and place a few at a time into the frying pan. Allow brochettes to fry, turning every 2 minutes or so until golden brown.

Transfer to paper towels then to serving plates. Garnish with a toast wedge, a lemon wedge, and parsley. *Serves 6.*

Note: Meunière Sauce is a beautiful complement to this dish.

OYSTER COCKTAIL

The word *cocktail* comes from the French *cocquetier*, which means "egg cup." The first cocktails were served in egg cups and the English-speaking Americans could not pronounce the word *cocquetier* properly, so eventually it became cocktail.

Because the oysters are served in a cocktail glass in this presentation, they are called cocktails.

1 cup cocktail sauce　　　　　　**1 lemon, cut into wedges**
2 dozen raw oysters

Arrange four 4-ounce chilled or frosted cocktail glasses with six oysters in the bottom of each. Pour 2 oz. of cocktail sauce over the oysters. Serve cold with lemon wedges. *Serves 4.*

BAKED OYSTERS AU GRATIN
ON THE HALF-SHELL

It was Antoine Alciatore—a nineteenth century immigrant from Marseilles who founded Antoine's Restaurant in 1840—who first began serving baked oysters in New Orleans. Although it would never have been done in France, the abundance of a single variety of oysters in Louisiana called for preparations that varied their presentation and taste. At one time, there were so many oyster vendors in New Orleans that it became necessary to license them in an effort to restrict their number.

Oysters remain a principal ingredient in many Creole dishes. This simple au gratin dish is most enjoyable to the palate.

2 cups rock salt
12 oyster half-shells
1 dozen raw oysters in their water
½ cup clarified butter
2 tbsp. green onions
1 cup heavy cream
Salt to taste
Pinch white pepper

1½ tbsp. finely grated Parmesan cheese
1 tbsp. beurre manie (½ tbsp. each of butter and flour kneaded together)
1 egg yolk
2 tbsp. fine bread crumbs
2 lemon wedges

Preheat oven to 400 degrees. Cover the bottoms of two 12-inch pie pans with rock salt. Arrange six half-oyster shells in a circle in each pan.

In a saucepan, poach the oysters in their own water until firm, about 5 minutes. Remove the pan from the heat and using a slotted spoon transfer the oysters onto their individual half-shells. Reserve the remaining liquid for the sauce.

In another saucepan, add 2 tbsp. of the clarified butter and gently sauté the green onions on a low heat until tender. Add the remaining oyster water. Bring to a simmer and add the heavy cream. Season to taste with salt and white pepper. Allow to slowly simmer for about 5 minutes. Add 1 tbsp. of the finely grated Parmesan cheese to the mixture, blend well, then add 1 tbsp. beurre manie. This will thicken the sauce to the correct consistency.

Remove the pan from the heat and whisk in the yolk of one egg. Spoon out equal amounts of the sauce onto the oysters, fully covering their tops (about 1 tbsp. each). Combine the bread crumbs with the remaining ½ tbsp. Parmesan and sprinkle it lightly over the sauced oysters. Dribble the oysters with the rest of the clarified butter. Transfer to the preheated oven and bake for 15 minutes, or until lightly browned and the sauce is bubbling. Remove from the oven and garnish with a lemon wedge. *Serves 2.*

Note: You can put the sauce into a pastry bag with a fluted tip to cover the oysters in a more decorative manner.

OYSTER PAN ROAST

This is a delicious way to conserve the luscious juices of the oysters so that they will be incorporated into the other ingredients as they all simmer together and roast in the oven.

Although I serve this dish as an appetizer, it would serve well as an entrée with just a small salad and a loaf of hot French bread to soak up the pan juices.

2 cups water	Pinch bay leaf powder
2 dozen oysters in their water	Salt to taste
2 tbsp. clarified butter	1/8 tsp. white pepper
1/3 cup finely chopped green onions	2 egg yolks
2 tbsp. flour	2 tbsp. fine bread crumbs mixed with 1 tsp. grated
Pinch thyme	Parmesan cheese

Preheat oven to 350 degrees. In a small pot, bring the water to a boil. Add the oysters in their liquid and boil until the edges curl (about 5 minutes). Remove the oysters using a slotted spoon and arrange six oysters in each of four individual casserole dishes. Reserve liquid for sauce.

In a large saucepan, sauté the green onions in the clarified butter until tender over a medium heat setting. Sprinkle in flour while constantly stirring with a wooden spoon until roux is hot. Gradually pour in oyster liquid and stir until sauce thickens. Season with thyme, bay leaf powder, salt, and white pepper. Remove from heat, stir in egg yolks, then cover each portion of oysters with sauce.

Sprinkle with the bread crumb/cheese mixture and bake for 15-20 minutes. *Serves 4.*

Note: This recipe is also included in Fish and Seafood.

OYSTERS REMOULADE

As you will find as you move through this book (that is, if you don't already know), we use many of the same preparations with many variations. That is, if we like the original to start.

Remoulade is one of New Orleans' best-known and best-loved dishes. It also comes in shrimp, crabmeat, and any other seafood you find palatable.

1 cup Remoulade Sauce
2 dozen raw oysters on the
   half-shell

2 lemons, quartered

Prepare the Remoulade Sauce and allow to stand refrigerated for 1 day. Arrange the oysters on the half-shell, six to a tray with equal portions of sauce in a cocktail dish in the center of the oysters. Serve cold with a lemon wedge. *Serves 4.*

OYSTERS ROCKEFELLER

Oysters Rockefeller, invented at Antoine's, have become known worldwide and are of the dishes that for many years have been known as "continental." Each chef has his own version....This is mine.

3 dozen large oysters
3 cups chopped spinach
½ cup finely chopped green onions
½ cup finely chopped yellow onions
⅓ cup finely chopped parsley
1 rib chopped celery
1 tsp. minced garlic
Pinch ground thyme
Pinch ground anise

¼ tsp. salt
¼ tsp. white pepper
¼ tsp. black pepper
1 tbsp. red wine vinegar
1 tsp. Worcestershire sauce
2 tbsp. herbsaint
1 cup clarified butter
1 cup fine French bread crumbs
6 cups rock salt
6 lemon wedges

Preheat oven to 350 degrees. In a small pot fill with water to cover oysters. Simmer for 5 minutes over medium-high heat. Drain and set aside.

To make the Rockefeller sauce, in a food processor combine the spinach, green onions, yellow onions, parsley, celery, garlic, thyme, anise, salt, white pepper, black pepper, red wine vinegar, Worcestershire, herbsaint, and butter. Coarsely puree the above ingredients. Transfer to a mixing bowl then fold in bread crumbs, blending well.

Arrange six 8-inch cake pans, fill each with rock salt to cover bottoms. Arrange 6 oyster half-shells in each. Place one oyster in each shell. Fill a pastry bag with Rockefeller sauce. Pipe equal portions of sauce over each shell. Place in the oven and bake for 25 minutes.

Remove and transfer pans to napkin-covered serving plates. Garnish with lemon wedges. *Serves 6.*

SHRIMP CANAPE ST. BARTS

The Caribbean Island of Saint Barthelemy, or St. Bart's as it is called, has a culinary history not unlike our own. The Spanish and French who settled there brought with them their own European cuisine that was then simmered in the pots of the Indians of the Islands—the Arawaks, Tainos, and Caribs—who introduced the use of local products, products that the Europeans had never seen before. Saint Barthelemy, by the way, was the patron saint and name of the brother of Columbus, after whom the island is named.

This is a recipe that I developed after one particular stay in St. Bart's, after a memorable evening in a restaurant there that served both Caribbean and French cuisine.

3 tbsp. finely ground bread crumbs	2 cups chopped raw shrimp
1 tbsp. finely grated Parmesan cheese	1 cup Béchamel Sauce
	2 tbsp. dry white wine
4 tbsp. clarified butter	3 egg yolks
4 tbsp. finely chopped green onions	4 slices whole wheat bread
	1 lemon, quartered
	2 tbsp. finely chopped parsley

In a small bowl, thoroughly combine the 3 tbsp. of finely ground bread crumbs with 1 tbsp. finely grated Parmesan cheese.

In a sauté pan on low heat, sauté the chopped green onions in 2 tbsp. of the clarified butter until tender. Add the chopped shrimp and lightly sauté until they are pink and firm (about 3 minutes). Fold in 1 cup Béchamel Sauce along with the dry white wine. Mix well then combine the yolks of 3 eggs and blend evenly. Remove from the heat and set aside.

Toast the bread then cut off the crusts and trim the remaining toast into rounds. Arrange the toast on a baking sheet and spoon equal amounts of the mixture onto each canapé with a uniform, rounded shape. Sprinkle on the remaining bread crumb mixture atop each canapé then dot with remaining clarified butter. Place the baking sheet into the oven on the broil setting for 5 minutes, or until golden brown.

Remove and garnish each serving with a lemon wedge and chopped parsley. *Serves 4.*

SHRIMP COCKTAIL

The fact that we call this presentation a cocktail comes from the same etymology as the word *cocktail*, as an alcoholic mixed drink.

It was in New Orleans that the pharmacist Amedee Peychaud began serving his homemade remedy for "all that ails ya," in particular, stomach disorders. His tonic was called "bitters." In order to make the taking of the remedy more pleasant to bear, Amedee began mixing the tonic with a jigger of Cognac and serving the preparation in an egg cup, or *coquetier*. An egg cup is that small vessel that is used to hold a soft-boiled egg upright so it can be eaten out of the shell.

This first preparation began to be called not bitters and Cognac, but a cocktail, which is a mispronunciation of the word *coquetier*, and anything served in the coquetier became a cocktail. It was not long before all mixed drinks became know as cocktails.

Shrimp, crab, and oyster cocktails take their name from the fact that they were originally, and sometimes still are, served in a glass that might be used for the service of cocktails.

1 cup cocktail sauce　　　　　　**1 lemon, cut into wedges**
2 dozen jumbo shrimp, boiled,
**　　peeled, and deveined (leave**
**　　tail fan on shrimp)**

Arrange four cocktail supremes or four 4-ounce chilled cocktail glasses. Fill each with 2 oz. of cocktail sauce. Arrange the boiled shrimp in an orderly fashion surrounding the sauce. Serve chilled with a lemon wedge. *Serves 4.*

SHRIMP MAISON

Although I also have in this grouping a recipe for Crabmeat Maison, this preparation is here as a popular dish that can be served as a light entrée as well as an appetizer. And since shrimp are generally easier to come by than lump crabmeat—as well as being less expensive—this dish is the one more often served.

½ tsp. lemon juice
1 level tbsp. Creole mustard
¾ cup mayonnaise
Salt to taste
Pinch cayenne pepper
Pinch white pepper
½ cup finely chopped green
    onions

1 tbsp. capers
1 tbsp. finely chopped parsley
1 lb. peeled, boiled medium
    shrimp
French bread, cut into rounds
    and toasted

In a medium mixing bowl, combine the lemon juice, Creole mustard, mayonnaise, salt, peppers, green onions, capers, and chopped parsley. Using a wire whisk, mix well. Fold in the shrimp until mixture is well blended. Refrigerate covered for 1 hour. Serve on toasted French bread rounds. *Serves 4.*

SHRIMP REMOULADE

This is a classic of Creole cuisine. Often, local residents will judge a restaurant by the way it prepares this dish. I am certain that if you were to judge my work by this preparation, you would find it all quite satisfactory.

1 bunch parsley, stems removed	1 tsp. Tabasco sauce
2 ribs celery	1 tsp. Worcestershire sauce
2 cloves garlic	Salt to taste
1 tbsp. minced bell pepper	¼ tsp. black pepper
1 cup Creole mustard	Pinch cayenne pepper
4 tbsp. paprika	1 pt. salad oil
2 tbsp. prepared horseradish	4 cups shredded lettuce
1 cup red wine vinegar	2 lb. shrimp, boiled and peeled
	2 lemons, quartered

Using a food processor, chop the parsley, celery, garlic, and bell pepper to a coarse puree. Transfer this to a large mixing bowl. Add the mustard, paprika, horseradish, vinegar, Tabasco, Worcestershire, salt, black pepper, and cayenne pepper. Using a wire whisk, beat constantly, adding small amounts of oil at a dribble until the sauce achieves a smooth consistency. Transfer to refrigerator to marinate for 24 hours.

To serve, place small amounts of shredded lettuce onto each chilled salad plate. Place equal amounts of shrimp over lettuce. Stir sauce and spoon over shrimp. Garnish with lemon wedges. *Serves 8.*

SHRIMP REMOULADE BLANC

There are more than a single type of remoulade sauces. This Remoulade Blanc, or white remoulade, is closer to the preparation of the classic French Remoulade, than that of the classic Creole Remoulade.

1¾ cups White Remoulade Sauce (Remoulade Blanc)	2 cups shredded lettuce
1 lb. jumbo shrimp, boiled and peeled	2 tomatoes, cut into 8 wedges

In a medium mixing bowl, fold the shrimp into the Remoulade Blanc, and allow to stand refrigerated for 2 hours. Restir and serve cold over shredded lettuce. Garnish each serving with 2 tomato wedges. *Serves 4.*

Soups and Stocks

BOUILLABAISSE

Much of the cuisine that is ours today began with the seed of French/Mediterranean cooking. The masterpiece of that cuisine, its *chef d'oeuvre*, is bouillabaisse. In New Orleans, we are blessed with a profundity of seafood. The richness of the seafood products that come from the Gulf of Mexico's waters and that of our own Lake Pontchartrain is a joy to any chef.

In this, my own New Orleans version of the French classic, trout and grouper are used. The pure white fleshiness of these marvelous fish contributes to a resulting dish that rivals—and may even excel over—its Mediterranean predecessor.

½ cup olive oil
1 cup finely chopped yellow onion
1 cup finely chopped green onion
3 whole tomatoes, skinned and chopped
5 cups Fish Stock
1 cup oyster water
½ cup white wine
Zest and juice of ½ lemon
Zest and juice of ½ orange
2 cloves garlic, minced
½ tsp. dried thyme
2 bay leaves

1 tbsp. paprika
Salt to taste
½ tsp. freshly ground black pepper
Pinch cayenne pepper
Generous pinch saffron
2 8-oz. trout filets (skin on)
2 8-oz. grouper filets (skin on)
12 peeled jumbo shrimp
12 large raw oysters, shelled, in their own water
1 tbsp. minced parsley
16 French bread croutons or toasted rounds

Heat ⅓ cup olive oil in a 12-inch shallow pot. Add 1 cup finely chopped yellow onions and sauté until tender. Add 1 cup finely chopped green onions and sauté together for another couple of minutes. Add the chopped tomatoes and simmer on medium heat for 5 minutes. Pour in the Fish Stock and the oyster water. Add white wine, the zest and the juice of the lemon and orange. Add the garlic, thyme, bay leaves, paprika, salt to taste, black pepper, cayenne pepper, and saffron. Cover and slowly simmer for 50 minutes, stirring from time to time.

Halve each fish filet and arrange in the sauce pot. Add the shrimp and oysters. Cover and cook for an additional 20 minutes. Do not stir. This will ensure the fish filets remain intact. Remove from the fire and sprinkle the parsley into pot.

To serve, arrange one piece of trout and one of grouper in each of four soup bowls. Using a slotted spoon, add 3 oysters and 3 shrimp to each bowl. Pour the remaining sauce liquid into each bowl. Serve with four toasted French bread croutons or rounds per bowl. *Serves 4.*

CONSOMME

Who doesn't have a desire from time to time for a simply delicious consommé? Although it is all too often relegated to the table of the ill, a good consommé is as rich and savory as any soup can be.

Remember that the secret to the preparation of consommé is a good stock. If you use the recipe in this book for Brown Stock, you will have a resulting worthwhile effort.

8 cups Brown Stock, chilled	**2 oz. very lean meat (veal)**
1 carrot, quartered	**Salt to taste**
⅓ cup chopped leeks	**2 egg whites and shells**
2 tbsp. finely chopped parsley	

Prepare and chill Brown Stock.

Degrease stock by skimming surface, removing any fat and grease particles. In a medium-sized pot, bring the stock barely to a boil. Add vegetables and meat and salt to taste. When the stock returns to a simmer, add the egg whites and shells. Partially cover and allow to gently simmer for one hour with an occasional stir. Do not allow the stock to boil—otherwise the consommé will not come clear.

Line a collander or sieve with several layers of cheese cloth or a clean white cotton cloth. Slowly ladle the stock through to filter out the egg and excess fat particles. *Makes 1 quart.*

FISH SOUP WITH POTATOES

Basic to almost every world cuisine is a simple, yet hearty fish soup. This recipe can be made with any fish that you might have more readily available than redfish, and the shrimp can be replaced with crabmeat, scallops, lobster pieces, oysters, etc.

For some reason, this soup is especially delicious when you make it with fish that you have caught yourself, on the same night as the fishing trip. Somehow the pleasure of enjoying your own catch at the table pursuant to the fishing expedition itself is noticeably heightened.

1 5-lb. red snapper	1 lemon
1 lb. shrimp (16-21 count)	2 potatoes
2 small yellow onions	2½ qt. water
2 peeled tomatoes	2 bay leaves
1 bell pepper	Salt to taste
1 carrot	Pepper to taste
1 rib celery	2 cups cooked rice

Filet the red snapper, reserving the head and bones. Cut filets into eight pieces of equal size and set aside.

Peel shrimp, reserving the heads and shells.

Quarter each onion as well as tomatoes. Cut the bell pepper into 2-inch squares and the carrot into julienne slices. Cut the celery rib into 4-inch pieces. Halve the lemon. Peel the potatoes and cut each into quarters.

Pour the water into a soup pot. Add fish head and bones as well as shrimp heads and peels. Add bay leaves and 1 of the quartered onions. Boil stock for 30 minutes.

Then into another soup pot retrieve liquid by passing stock through a fine sieve or strainer. Discard heads and shells.

Reheat stock, add remaining onion, tomatoes, bell pepper, carrot, lemon, and potatoes. Cook for 20 minutes then add shrimp and fish pieces. Add salt and pepper to taste.

After soup comes to a boil, cook for another 10 minutes. Each serving should contain one piece of fish, one piece of potato, two shrimp, and equal amounts of vegetables. Spoon 2 tbsp. rice into each bowl. *Serves 8.*

CHICKEN ANDOUILLE GUMBO

One of the most all-important dishes of our cookery is gumbo.

Now, a gumbo can be many different types. It can be seafood, chicken, oyster, duck. It can be filé or okra. It can be Creole or Cajun. The truth is that there are as many different gumbos as there are cooks in Louisiana.

This gumbo is a straightforward representation of one that is more commonplace and easy to assemble than some others might be, while it still delivers a fine example of the art of gumbo cooking.

¾ cup vegetable oil	1 gallon water
1 cup flour	1 tbsp. salt
2 2-lb. chickens	1 level tbsp. black pepper
1 yellow onion	1 tbsp. minced garlic
1 bunch green onions	½ cup chopped parsley
½ lb. andouille sausage	6 cups cooked rice
1 large tomato, peeled and crushed	

In a heavy skillet, prepare a roux by heating the oil over a medium heat setting. Sprinkle in flour while constantly stirring with a wire whisk. Continue cooking slowly until roux achieves a dark amber color. Put aside, stirring occasionally, as heat from skillet will continue cooking roux, and stirring will prevent sticking or scorching.

Quarter both chickens. Finely chop yellow and green onions and slice sausage into ⅛-inch slices. Peel and crush the tomato.

Fill a large pot with a gallon of water and season with salt and pepper. Add chopped onions, andouille, tomato, and garlic. Place chicken quarters into the pot and allow to boil for 20 minutes. Remove chicken from the pot, reserving stock. Remove chicken meat from carcass and return meat to pot. Allow stock to come to a rolling boil.

Gradually add the roux, stirring constantly until soup thickens. Reduce heat and simmer gumbo for 30 minutes. Add parsley and stir. Serve over rice. *Serves 12.*

OYSTER ARTICHOKE SOUP

Although this dish seems to have been on New Orleans menus forever, it was only some fifteen years ago that famed New Orleans chef and restaurateur Warren Leruth first put it on the menu of his most popular Leruth's Restaurant.

Leruth trained in many places to learn his craft, one of which was here at Galatoire's. I thank Warren for bringing the concept to us, although this recipe is a variation of my own.

2 large artichokes	2 cloves garlic, minced
Enough salted water to boil	4 tbsp. flour
artichokes	¼ tsp. ground thyme
5 cups water (for soup)	1 tsp. salt
15 oysters, in their water	¼ tsp. white pepper
2 bay leaves	2 tbsp. lemon juice
2 tbsp. butter	2 tbsp. chopped parsley
4 green onions, chopped	

Boil the artichokes in salted water for 30 minutes. Allow to cool, then peel the outer leaves, reserving a few to scrape the more tender part from. Also reserve the hearts and bottoms, removing the pulp from the bottoms. Cut the bottoms into thin slices as well as the hearts. Put aside.

In a pot add 5 cups of water and 15 oysters in their own water. Add the bay leaves and bring to a boil.

In a separate pot melt the butter and sauté the chopped green onions until tender. Add the minced garlic. Add the flour and blend well using a wire whisk. Pour in the stock containing the oysters. Continue stirring with a wisk until the soup thickens.

Remove 3 of the 15 oysters, chop fine, and return to the soup. Add the sliced artichoke bottoms and hearts. Season with thyme, salt, and pepper. Add the lemon juice and parsley. Simmer for 10 minutes and serve. *Serves 6.*

RED BEAN SOUP

If you haven't eaten the traditional Red Beans and Rice on Monday in New Orleans, you must never have visited here.

I like to take the dish one step further and I have refined it into a smooth, luscious soup.

1 lb. dried red kidney beans	½ tsp. white pepper
1 gallon water	⅛ tsp. ground thyme
2 ham hocks	2 bay leaves
1 yellow onion, chopped	1 tsp. parsley, finely chopped
3 toes garlic, minced	1 tsp. Tabasco sauce
2 ribs celery, chopped	1 cup ham, chopped
Salt to taste	

In a soup pot soak the red beans in water for 6 hours. Rinse beans, discarding soaking water. Add a gallon of fresh water and bring the beans to a boil over a medium heat setting. Add the ham hocks and season with onion, garlic, celery, salt, pepper, thyme, bay leaves, parsley, and Tabasco sauce. Allow to simmer 3 hours, adding additional stock or water to adjust consistency.

Press the mixture through a coarse sieve into another soup pot and heat as needed. Serve in bowls with a sprinkle of finely chopped ham in each. *Serves 10-12.*

SHRIMP SOUP VELOUTE

If you want to serve a smooth, rich, and mouth-watering soup that all your guests will rave over, serve Shrimp Soup Velouté.

The preparation is fashioned from the old school, where eggs and heavy cream were *de rigueur*, almost regulation.

2 cups shrimp
2 pt. Fish Stock or Fish Fumet
6 tbsp. flour
3 tbsp. clarified butter
1 rib celery, finely chopped
3 shallots, finely chopped
1 small carrot, finely chopped

Enough water to cover the
shrimp and vegetables
Salt to taste
⅛ tsp. cayenne pepper
2 egg yolks
½ cup cream

Peel and devein the shrimp. Reserve shells.

Prepare a Fish Stock or Fish Fumet using the shells from the shrimp. Prepare a white roux combining the flour and clarified butter. Blend well with a wire whisk. Thicken the Fish Stock with the roux. Allow the soup to simmer over a low heat setting while cooking the shrimp.

In a medium pot, heat the water for the shrimp and vegetables to a boil. Add the shrimp, vegetables, salt, and cayenne pepper. Allow to boil for 15 minutes. Strain the shrimp and vegetables from the liquid then press this mixture through a fine sieve or a food processor. Add this vegetable/shrimp puree to the soup and continue to simmer for 15 minutes.

Remove from the heat and whisk in two egg yolks and the cream. Serve hot. *Makes 4 servings.*

SEAFOOD GUMBO

This is the queen of Creole dishes and the king of gumbos. If there is a recipe that you should try as an introduction to understanding what New Orleans food is all about, this is the dish.

It is true that every New Orleans cook has his or her own recipe for gumbo, but this is a particularly exalted version. I guarantee you will love it.

½ cup vegetable oil
¾ cup flour
1 gallon of water or white stock
1 tbsp. salt
¼ tbsp. ground dried thyme
⅛ tsp. cayenne pepper
¼ tsp. white pepper
1 yellow onion, chopped
½ bell pepper, diced
2 ribs celery, chopped

1 lb. shrimp, chopped
1 tomato, peeled and crushed
2 tbsp. tomato puree
1 tbsp. minced garlic
1 dozen oysters in their water
2 cups sliced okra
1 lb. lump crabmeat
2 tbsp. chopped parsley
6 cups cooked rice

In a heavy skillet, prepare a roux by heating the vegetable oil on a medium heat setting. Sprinkle in the flour and stir constantly until the roux achieves a dark amber color. Put aside, stirring occasionally.

Fill a medium-sized pot with one gallon of water or white stock. Add salt, ground thyme, cayenne, and white pepper. Add chopped onion, bell pepper, and celery. Allow water or stock to come to a boil. Add chopped shrimp, crushed tomato, tomato puree, and minced garlic. Simmer for 20 minutes on a medium heat setting. Add the oysters in their water, then gradually add in the prepared roux. Stir until gumbo thickens. Add sliced okra and simmer for another 20 minutes. Add crabmeat and chopped parsley. Remove from heat and serve over rice. *Serves 10-12.*

SHRIMP BISQUE

Now, this is a true *specialité* of Creole cuisine. It carries all the essences of fine Creole cooking, including the fact that it takes a fair amount of time to prepare.

The addition of the Shrimp Balls, although not absolutely necessary, enhances the soup so measurably that you would not want to prepare the soup without going the distance to prepare the garnish.

2 qt. water	1 rib celery, chopped
Salt to taste	2 tbsp. flour
⅛ tsp. cayenne pepper	½ cup bread crumbs
2 lb. shrimp	⅛ tsp. thyme
2 tbsp. clarified butter	Salt to taste
1 medium yellow onion, chopped	White pepper to taste

In a soup pot, bring the water to a rolling boil. Season with salt and cayenne pepper. Boil the shrimp for 15 minutes. Strain the shrimp, reserving the stock for soup. Lay the shrimp out flat and allow to cool enough to handle.

Peel, devein, and rinse the shrimp, then chop or mince.

In a medium pot sauté the onions and celery in butter over medium low heat until tender. Add the flour, stirring constantly for about a minute. While stirring constantly, gradually add enough shrimp stock to achieve a soup-like texture. Reserve remaining liquid to adjust consistency.

When this mixture is well blended, add the minced shrimp and simmer for about 5 minutes, then add the bread crumbs and mix well. Remove from the heat, then strain through a sieve separating the liquid from the shrimp mixture. Reserve half the shrimp mixture for Shrimp Balls and return the other half to the soup pot.

Season the soup with thyme, salt, and white pepper. Puree, and transfer to an earthenware pot. Set aside.

SHRIMP BALLS

1 tbsp. clarified butter	2 tbsp. fine bread crumbs
½ cup finely chopped green onions	2 tbsp. of soup
½ shrimp mixture	1 egg yolk
	1 tbsp. finely chopped parsley

To make shrimp balls, preheat the oven to 350 degrees. Sauté green onions in butter until tender. Add reserved shrimp mixture and bread crumbs. Moisten with 2 tbsp. of the soup. Remove from the heat and blend in an egg yolk. Allow to cool enough to handle, then roll into small balls. Place on a greased baking sheet and bake for 10 minutes. Place the shrimp balls into the soup, reheat, and serve 3 shrimps balls per serving. Garnish with a sprinkle of parsley. *Serves 6-8.*

TURTLE SOUP

Turtle soup was a mainstay of New Orleans cuisine from the very beginning. Vendors in the marketplace offered a myriad of turtle varieties—tortoise, sea turtle, box turtle, snapping turtle, soft-shell turtle, and Mobilia. The most prized were the Green sea turtle, now on the endangered species list, and the soft-shell turtle.

Bienville, the founder of New Orleans, wrote in one of his missives to the ruling bodies in France that his favorite food was a soup made of the soft-shell turtle. The most curious thing about its preparation was that the soft shell of the turtle was employed and eaten along with the meat.

These days, a good-sized soft shell is a rare find and most highly prized by the country folk who know how to do it justice in the pot.

1 cup cooking oil	¼ tsp. cayenne pepper
2 ribs celery, chopped	1 tsp. white pepper
1 yellow onion, diced	1 tbsp. salt
½ bell pepper, diced	1 tsp. ground thyme
1 lb. turtle meat, ground	1 tbsp. minced garlic
2 tbsp. paprika	Juice of ½ lemon
⅔ cup flour	½ cup sherry wine
5 cups Brown Stock	2 hard-boiled eggs, sieved
1 tomato, crushed	2 tbsp. parsley, chopped
2 tbsp. tomato puree	

In a medium-sized pot (5-quart), heat the cooking oil on a medium-high heat setting. Add the celery, onion, bell pepper, and ground turtle meat. Stir and cook until the vegetables are transparent and turtle meat begins to brown.

Add paprika and flour, then stir to blend evenly. Add the Brown Stock, constantly stirring until the soup thickens. Add the crushed tomato and tomato puree and stir. Add cayenne and white peppers, salt, and thyme. Stir.

Add the garlic, the juice of ½ lemon, and sherry wine and continue to stir. Add the sieved hard-boiled eggs and parsley and stir. *Serves 8-10.*

BROWN STOCK

The secret to the soup or the sauce is the stock. If the stock is properly made, and maintains the depth of richness that you require to continue on with its inclusion in a recipe, than you can be assured that the recipe will be its best.

3 lb. lean meat (veal)
3 lb. cracked veal bones
2 large yellow onions, quartered
2 carrots, quartered
4 jumbo mushrooms
2 cups plus 8 qt. water
Bouquet Garni:
  1 bay leaf
  4 cloves garlic
  4 sprigs parsley
  ¼ tsp. thyme

2 ribs chopped celery
2 tsp. salt
1 tsp. black peppercorns

Preheat oven to 450 degrees. In a roasting pan place the meat, bones, and vegetables and put in the oven for 45 minutes, turning occasionally until evenly browned. Remove from the oven, drain off excess grease, and transfer ingredients to a large soup pot. Add 2 cups of the water to the roasting pan to deglaze it, then scrape the bottom of the pan.

Pass the liquid through a fine sieve into the soup pot containing the bones and vegetables. Fill the pot with enough water to cover the ingredients by 2 inches (about 8 quarts).

Prepare a bouquet garni with bay leaf, garlic, parsley, and thyme. Tie these up in cheese cloth and add it to the pot. Add celery, salt, and peppercorns and bring the liquid to a simmer. Partially cover and allow to simmer slowly over a low heat setting for 4-5 hours. Drain through a sieve. Refrigerate uncovered until cool. *Makes 3-4 quarts.*

FISH STOCK OR FISH FUMET

A sauce is only as good as the stock on which it is based. If you skimp on the fish fumet, or the poultry, veal, or beef stock, you will have a resulting sauce that is less than the best it can be.

Make your best effort to start with a good, rich stock and you will always be happy with the final result.

2 lb. fish heads, bones, and trimmings	½ tsp. whole cloves
2½ qt. cold water	2 bay leaves
2 medium onions, quartered	1 tbsp. salt
1 carrot, chopped	1 tsp. whole black peppercorns
1 rib celery, chopped	2 lemons, halved
	½ cup dry white wine

Rinse the fish head cavities, bones, and trimmings of excess blood with cold water. Place the carcass in a large pot and fill with cold water. Add all the remaining ingredients to the stock. Bring to a slow boil and allow to cook for one hour. Strain through a fine sieve. *Makes 4 cups.*

Note: Beginning the stock with cold water will allow a less cloudy result. Also, fish stock freezes beautifully as a helpful tool for future use.

Salads

GRAPEFRUIT SALAD

A very old New Orleans salad that used to be found in every restaurant was the grapefruit salad. The Mustard Vinaigrette makes the grapefruit a true salad, one especially to be enjoyed on hot August days when the heat becomes a bit intolerable.

MUSTARD VINAIGRETTE DRESSING

½ cup Dijon mustard
1 tbsp. red wine vinegar
½ cup salad oil

Salt to taste
Black pepper, freshly ground,
  to taste

4 grapefruit
1 head iceberg lettuce, washed,
  trimmed, and torn

In a small mixing bowl, combine the Dijon mustard with the red wine vinegar and gradually whisk in the salad oil at a dribble until it is completely absorbed in an emulsification.

Season to taste with salt and pepper and hold aside in the refrigerator to chill.

Peel the whole grapefruits, separate and trim each individual section, and arrange the sections in a fan design over torn lettuce leaves on well-chilled salad plates.

Serve with the Mustard Vinaigrette, garnish with a single red cherry, and serve. *Serves 4.*

GODCHAUX SALAD

Galatoire's has long served the Canal Street merchants, the Godchaux family being one of the finest. Although their store has departed from the neighborhood, we keep the memory of other times with the Godchaux salad, which was named after the illustrious department store and its founder, Leon Godchaux.

1 head iceberg lettuce, cored
    and cubed
2 large tomatoes, stems
    removed, cubed
1 lb. backfin lump crabmeat
30-35 large shrimp, boiled and
    peeled

⅔ cup salad oil
⅓ cup red wine vinegar
½ cup Creole mustard
3 hard-boiled eggs
12 anchovies

In a large salad bowl, combine the lettuce, tomatoes, crabmeat, and shrimp. In a small bowl, combine the oil, vinegar, and mustard and mix well with a wire whisk. Pour the dressing over the salad and toss.

Divide the salad onto six chilled plates (approximately 2 cups each). Garnish each salad with ½ of a sieved hard-boiled egg and 2 anchovies. *Serves 6.*

CARIBBEAN CHICKEN SALAD WITH ORANGE AND BALSAMIC VINEGAR

This is a delightful salad that can make the dog days of summer a time for enjoying something light and healthful.

Another of my inventions created after a similar dish that I was able to enjoy during an excursion to the Caribbean, this makes a hot afternoon meal that is just right for the heat.

4 6-oz. boneless, skinless, half
chicken breasts
1 cup 2 tbsp. olive oil (reserve
½ cup for Dressing)
⅛ tsp. cayenne pepper
2 qt. (½ gallon or 8 cups) rough
chopped mixed lettuces: red
oak leaf, romaine, Belgian
endive; or 1 head Belgian
endive

1 large tomato, diced
1 bell pepper, diced
1 red pepper, diced
1 yellow pepper, diced
1 tsp. dried tarragon
Salt to taste
Pepper, freshly ground, to taste

Lightly coat each chicken breast with olive oil, using about 2 tbsp. of the oil. Lightly season with cayenne pepper and grill over embers for about 4 minutes on each side, or until cooked through. Transfer to side plate.

In a large salad bowl, combine the three lettuces, diced tomato, and peppers. Season with salt, pepper, and tarragon. Pour dressing over salad and toss.

Divide salad equally onto four large chilled plates or wide soup bowls. Slice half chicken breasts diagonally. Flan each chicken breast half and place atop each salad. *Makes 4 entrée salads.*

DRESSING

¾ cup orange juice, freshly
squeezed
3 tbsp. balsamic vinegar
2 tbsp. grated orange peel,
orange skin only

½ cup olive oil (reserve from
above list of ingredients)

Combine orange juice, balsamic vinegar, and grated orange peel in a mixing bowl. Gradually whisk in ½ cup of the oil.

WARM POTATO SALAD LYONNAISE

Many of the early merchants, those who sold the meat and produce in the French Market of New Orleans Vieux Carré, were of Lyon-French extraction. These bold pioneers who came to this morass of land were the backbone of the community.

The famous cuisine of Lyon, one of France's most revered cuisines, was incorporated into the Creole pot. This simple potato dish, however, underwent few changes. Its simplicity is its essence.

4 medium potatoes	**Salt to taste**
Enough salted water to cover	**White pepper to taste**
2 medium yellow onions	**1 tsp. finely chopped parsley**
½ cup clarified butter	

Place potatoes in a pot filled with salted water to cover. Boil for 25 minutes. Drain into a colander and allow to cool. Peel potatoes using a butter knife. Slice each potato in half lengthwise, then slice each half across into thin semicircular slices.

Peel and cut the ends from each onion. Place on flat ends and cut in half. Then cut the halves into julienne slices.

In a large sauté pan, heat 4 tbsp. of the clarified butter on a medium setting and sauté onions until translucent. Remove and drain off excess butter. Put aside.

In a separate sauté pan, heat remaining butter on a medium heat setting and sauté the potato slices until they are light brown. Salt and pepper to taste.

Fold in the onions and continue to sauté the combination for 2 minutes. Remove onto serving plates. Garnish with a sprinkle of parsley. *Serves 4.*

Note: This recipe is also included in Vegetables as Potatoes Lyonnaise.

FRESH TUNA SALAD

As simple as it is, if this is not a grand departure from the mundane tuna salad … nothing is.

Of course, any fish can be used in the place of the tuna. Just use whatever is fresh and available.

1 lb. fresh tuna meat
Enough water to cover
Salt to taste
1 bay leaf
Juice of 1 lemon
¼ cup celery, finely chopped
¼ cup green onions, finely
   chopped

1 tsp. fresh chopped parsley
2 tbsp. mayonnaise
1 tsp. Creole mustard
1 head butter lettuce, rinsed
   and outer leaves removed
1 pickle, cut into 4 wedges
1 lemon, cut into 4 wedges

Place tuna in a pot with enough water to cover. Bring the water to a boil then season with salt and bay leaf. Add lemon juice and poach tuna for 15 minutes. Remove and allow to cool. Refrigerate for 1 hour. In a large stainless steel bowl, separate the tuna into flakes using a fork.

Add the celery, green onions, and parsley to the flaked tuna. Fold in the mayonnaise and Creole mustard until blended well. Return to the refrigerator for 1 hour to chill.

Place one whole leaf of butter lettuce on each of four chilled salad plates then spoon equal portions of tuna salad atop each. Garnish with a pickle wedge and a lemon wedge. *Serves 4.*

CELERY RIBS STUFFED WITH ASPARAGUS AND BLUE CHEESE

Simple as this may seem, hot summer meals in New Orleans often call for simple fare and cool tasty tidbits to complement cocktails before dinner.

The crispness of the celery, the tastiness of the asparagus, and the smooth saltiness of the blue cheese meld well together for this purpose.

16 asparagus
1 head celery (approximately 8 ribs)
1 small yellow onion, minced
1 cup blue cheese, crumbled
Salt to taste
¼ tsp. white pepper, or to taste
½ cup whipping cream

In a medium pot, blanch the asparagus tips in enough salted water to cover for 3 minutes.

Trim the celery ribs under cold water, slice each rib in half crosswise.

In a medium mixing bowl, combine the minced onion, crumbled blue cheese, salt, pepper, and whipping cream. Fold mixture until thoroughly blended. Refrigerate mixture to chill for 30 minutes.

Trim the celery ribs and asparagus to equal lengths. Place one asparagus tip into each trimmed celery rib and top with the blue cheese mixture. Chill to serve. *Makes 16 pieces.*

Note: This recipe is also included as an appetizer.

STUFFED AVOCADO WITH CRABMEAT

It was the Spanish who introduced the avocado to New Orleans. Although it was a popular indigenous fruit of Mexico to the Andean regions long before the Spanish conquest, it was in the West Indies where the fruit was first discovered by the Spanish. It was also the Spanish who introduced the concept of "salad."

In this dish, a most popular dish with New Orleans' regular customers, avocado is combined with our famous Creole tomato and our succulent crabmeat. The touch of Creole mustard adds the "bite" that makes it work together so well.

3 large ripe avocadoes	2 tbsp. Creole mustard
1 lb. lump crabmeat	4 tbsp. mayonnaise
2 large tomatoes, peeled, seed- ed, and diced	1 tsp. lemon juice Salt to taste
2 eggs, hard-boiled and sliced	Pepper to taste
2 green onions, finely chopped	6 fresh lemon slices
2 sprigs parsley, finely chopped	

Halve the avocadoes and remove the seeds. With a spoon, carefully remove the meat, leaving the entire half-shell intact.

Dice the avocado meat and place in a bowl with the crabmeat, tomatoes, egg slices, onions, parsley, Creole mustard, mayonnaise, and lemon juice. Salt and pepper to taste.

Fold mixture together well.

Fill the avocado shells with the mixture and serve chilled, using lemon slices for garnish. *Serves 6.*

SABA SEA SALAD

On another perfect day in the island paradise of Saba, I was asked to make the salad for a group dining with restaurant friends in a local favored establishment. Surprisingly, that day, the restaurant owner had just received a shipment of fresh crabmeat and shrimp and was anxious to let me use them for the creation. This salad was the result.

I brought the recipe home and often serve this dish as either a salad course of a larger meal, or as a meal by itself. The quality of the ingredients is primary here.

⅔ cup Creole mustard
1 cup salad oil
4 tbsp. red wine vinegar
1 lb. large lump crabmeat
18 large shrimp, boiled and
   peeled

2 tomatoes, cubed
1 head iceberg lettuce, cubed
1 hard-boiled egg, sieved
6 anchovy filets

In a small mixing bowl, combine the Creole mustard, salad oil, and red wine vinegar. Mix together well with a wire whisk.

In a large salad bowl, combine the crabmeat, shrimp, tomatoes, and lettuce. Pour the mustard/vinegar dressing over salad and toss until mixture is evenly blended. Divide onto six well-chilled salad plates and garnish with a sprinkle of sieved egg and 1 filet of anchovy on each. *Serves 6.*

SPINACH SALAD
WITH WHITE REMOULADE SAUCE

The spinach salad is something that has come into vogue during my lifetime. I have taken it a step further and used one of the grand Creole sauces as a dressing.

1 cup White Remoulade Sauce
¼ lb. bacon, cut into 1-inch
  squares
1 10-oz. bag fresh spinach,
  washed and trimmed

Salt to taste
¼ tsp. black pepper, freshly
  ground
2 hard-boiled eggs, halved

Prepare White Remoulade Sauce, cover, and refrigerate to chill.

In a medium skillet, fry bacon pieces until crisp. Transfer to paper towels to drain.

In a large salad bowl, add the spinach leaves, season with salt and pepper, and toss with the Remoulade Sauce. Place equal portions on chilled salad plates, garnish with the bacon and ½ hard-boiled egg per serving. *Serves 4.*

ASPARAGUS SALAD VINAIGRETTE

The color combination of both the green and the white asparagus make for an attractive salad plate. It is not necessary, however. One or the other will do if both are not available.

1 dozen green asparagus spears
1 dozen white asparagus spears
Enough water to cover
⅛ tsp. salt
2 tbsp. balsamic vinegar

6 tbsp. olive oil
3 tbsp. shallots, finely chopped
2 cloves minced garlic
1 tsp. finely chopped parsley
8 tomato wedges

Tie the asparagus spears in bunches of 12. Blanch in boiling water for 2 minutes. Remove and allow to cool. Wrap in plastic paper and refrigerate.

In a small mixing bowl, prepare a vinaigrette dressing by dissolving the salt in the vinegar. Gradually whisk in the oil at a dribble until the mixture emulsifies. Add the shallots, garlic, and parsley. Cover and refrigerate for 30 minutes.

To serve, place 3 white asparagus staggered with 3 green on each chilled salad plate. Mix or shake dressing in a bottle and pour over asparagus. Garnish with a wedge of tomato on each side of the plate. *Serves 4.*

GRILLED CHICKEN ROMAINE WITH MANGO COMPOTE

This simple salad composed of grilled chicken tenders, fruit, and romaine lettuce leaves is a delightful calorie-wise choice for a warm summer's day luncheon.

I first created this dish while anchored off the famous Baths at Virgin Gorda, after a morning of snorkeling and exploring this intriguing location. Its highly unusual rock formations roll down into the azure blue water like a smooth frozen splash of lava.

2 heads romaine lettuce
Enough ice water to cover
4 skinless chicken breast filets

Salt to taste
Black pepper to taste

MANGO COMPOTE

1 cup sugar
1½ cups water

2 cups mango, peeled, seeded, and cubed

For the Mango Compote, dissolve the sugar in the water in a saucepan, heating and stirring until a syrup forms. Cook the cubed mango in the syrup for 15 minutes. Allow to cool. Refrigerate for the finished garnish.

Cut stalk ends from lettuce. Discard outermost leaves and select the inner or less mature leaves for your salad. Soak leaves in ice water for 5 minutes and pat dry.

Trim chicken breasts of all excess fat and cut each into four lengthwise strips to fashion with the romaine leaves.

Season chicken tenders and lightly grill on a medium heat setting or flame for about 2 minutes on each side. Baste with some of the Mango Compote.

Arrange four romaine leaves in a circular fashion on each of four chilled salad plates. Garnish with 2-3 tbsp. of cold Mango Compote in the center of each salad. *Serves 4.*

CRAWFISH SALAD

It is easy for us in New Orleans to devise many dishes that rely on the succulent crustacean, crawfish, because they are so plentiful. In other areas of the country where these delicious morsels cannot be had, this same dish, as well as any other dishes made from crawfish, can be made from shrimp, crabmeat, scallops, lobster, or even nuggets of fish filet.

In any of these other cases where a substitution can be made, it is necessary to begin the recipe with a cooked product.

1 head romaine lettuce	4 finely chopped green onions
1 lb. crawfish tails	2 tsp. finely chopped parsley
4 tbsp. mayonnaise	2 tsp. capers
2 tsp. Creole mustard	Black pepper to taste
2 tbsp. lemon juice	1 lemon, quartered
1 oz. white wine	

Cut the stalk ends from the lettuce. Discard outermost leaves and select four young tender ones for the salad bed. Soak leaves in ice water for 5 minutes, then pat dry.

In a mixing bowl, combine crawfish tails, mayonnaise, mustard, lemon juice, wine, green onions, parsley, capers, and pepper. Simply mix together well and chill.

To serve, place a lettuce leaf on each chilled salad plate. Spoon equal amounts of mixture onto each bed. Garnish with a lemon wedge. *Serves 4.*

MIXED GREEN SALAD
WITH GARLIC VINAIGRETTE

This is a variation of a salad that has been a New Orleans classic for a very long time. The balsamic vinegar, which is made from sherry as opposed to another less sweet wine, gives it just that slightest sweetness that melds the other flavors together so well with the garlic.

1 head romaine lettuce	2 cloves garlic, minced
1 head red oak lettuce	3 tbsp. finely chopped green
1 head round or butter lettuce	onions
¼ tsp. salt	1 cup small croutons
1 tbsp. balsamic vinegar	¼ tsp. black pepper, freshly
6 tbsp. olive oil	ground

Wash and drain all three varieties of lettuce. Beginning with the romaine, peel and discard the outer leaves and select the inner most or heart of the lettuce. Chop into bite-sized pieces and place in a large salad bowl. Do the same with the red oak and butter leaves. Refrigerate covered with plastic wrap.

Prepare a vinaigrette dressing in a small mixing bowl by dissolving the salt in the balsamic vinegar. Gradually whisk in the oil at a dribble until the mixture emulsifies. Add the garlic and green onions. Chill covered for 30 minutes.

When ready to serve, shake the dressing well and pour over the salad. Toss and serve on chilled plates. Garnish with croutons, and finish with the pepper. *Serves 4-6.*

SALAD MAISON WITH MUSTARD VINAIGRETTE DRESSING

Sometimes our rather hearty dinners require a light salad, yet we still want a flavor that gives us a proper bite. This Mustard Vinaigrette does just that and complements especially meat entrées.

MUSTARD VINAIGRETTE DRESSING

½ cup Dijon mustard
1 tbsp. red wine vinegar
½ cup salad oil

Salt to taste
Black pepper, freshly ground,
   to taste

1 head red leaf letuce
1 Belgian endive, diced

1 head romaine

In a small mixing bowl, combine the Dijon mustard with the red wine vinegar and gradually whisk in the salad oil at a dribble until it is completely absorbed in an emulsification.

Season to taste with salt and pepper and hold aside in the refrigerator to chill.

Wash and dry the lettuces and tear into bite-sized pieces. Place them in a salad bowl, toss with the vinaigrette, and serve. *Serves 6.*

HEARTS OF ROMAINE SALAD WITH PAPAYA AND BALSAMIC VINEGAR DRESSING

Papaya is another of my fond memories from the Caribbean. In this dressing, it adds a sweetness and an island flavor with the underlying taste of the nutmeg that is quite unique.

1 head romaine lettuce	Salt to taste
1 small ripe papaya	Pepper to taste
1 tbsp. balsamic vinegar	Pinch cayenne
3 tbsp. salad oil	⅛ tsp. nutmeg

Wash and dry the romaine lettuce. Select the innermost tender leaves. Arrange them attractively on two well-chilled salad plates. Hold aside in the refrigerator.

Peel, seed, and mince the papaya.

In a medium mixing bowl, combine the balsamic vinegar and oil, season with salt and pepper to taste, add a pinch of cayenne and the ground nutmeg. Whisk vigorously until well blended. Fold in the minced papaya and spoon the dressing over the romaine leaves. *Serves 2.*

CRAB AVOCADO SALAD

The marvelous fact that we have delicious crabmeat available almost all year long allows us the luxury of using it in many differing dishes.

In this dish, the crab has already been boiled or steamed. Chilled, it adds the ultimate garnish to the avocado, an introduction of the Spanish to New Orleans and salad mixture.

DRESSING

| ¼ cup Creole mustard | ½ cup peanut oil |
| ¼ cup red wine vinegar | |

In a small mixing bowl, combine the Creole mustard, red wine vinegar, and gradually whisk in the peanut oil at a dribble until all is emulsified.

SALAD INGREDIENTS

1 head of iceberg lettuce,
  washed and torn into pieces
2 medium tomatoes, cubed
2 ripe avocadoes, seeded,
  skinned, and cubed

1 lb. lump crabmeat
1 hard-boiled egg, sieved
8 anchovy filets
1 lemon, quartered

In a medium salad bowl, combine the iceberg lettuce with the tomatoes, avocado cubes, crabmeat, and sieved hard-boiled egg. Toss with the Dressing. Place equal portions on chilled salad plates. Garnish each plate with a cross of 2 anchovy filets and a lemon wedge. *Serves 4.*

STUFFED CREOLE TOMATO WITH SHRIMP

Because we have the absolute joy of having what some consider the best tomato grown in the world, the Creole tomato, we have invented more than many ways to use them. They have become salads, accompaniments, and entrées. They are baked, fried, stuffed, and smothered.

We will stuff a good Creole tomato with any other of our good products. Shrimp, for example, make an excellent stuffing. But even we find ourselves without the "best" on occasion and will use whatever tomato is available.

4 medium tomatoes
32 jumbo shrimp, boiled,
  peeled, and deveined

4 tbsp. mayonnaise
2 tsp. Creole mustard
4 bay leaves

Wash and core the tomatoes. Slice each tomato into eighths halfway down vertically. Arrange 8 shrimp per tomato between the slices.

In a mixing bowl, combine the mayonnaise with the Creole mustard, mix well, and spoon this mixture into the center of each tomato. Garnish with a bay leaf and serve cold. *Serves 4.*

STUFFED CREOLE TOMATO WITH GRILLED CHICKEN

Just as with the shrimp stuffing, I have made this salad into an entrée if you wish. The tomato needs to be properly ripe, and the grilled flavor of the chicken is measurably important.

4 chicken breasts, skinless, boneless, and halved
4 tbsp. oil
1 tbsp. Creole mustard
1 clove garlic, minced

1 tsp. finely chopped parsley
4 medium tomatoes
4 tbsp. mayonnaise, homemade or prepared
2 tsp. Creole mustard

Preheat the grill.

Slice the chicken breasts into 2 x 4-inch finger pieces. In a small mixing bowl, mix the oil at a dribble with the Creole mustard using a wire whisk. Add the garlic and parsley. Dredge the chicken through this mixture. Place chicken on the grill to cook for about 2 minutes on each side. Remove from the heat and hold aside.

Wash and core the tomatoes. Slice each tomato into eighths from the tops halfway down to the base. Arrange the grilled chicken slices between each tomato slice (8 per tomato). Combine the mayonnaise and Creole mustard in a small mixing bowl and spoon this mixture into the center of each tomato. Serve chilled. *Serves 4.*

Vegetables

ASPARAGUS AU GRATIN

Not one of the vegetables that you see prepared this way as often as potatoes or cauliflower, asparagus lends itself well to this preparation.

When asparagus are in season and can be had as often as you might want, varied preparations like this one are welcomed in the kitchen and in the dining room.

1 dozen asparagus tips	**Pinch cayenne pepper**
2 cups Béchamel Sauce	**⅛ tsp. white pepper**
2 cups grated cheddar cheese	**Mixture of 2 tbsp. fine bread**
½ cup half & half cream	**crumbs and 1 tbsp. grated**
2 egg yolks	**Parmesan cheese**
Salt to taste	**2 tbsp. clarified butter**

Steam the asparagus tips for 3 minutes then cut into bite-sized pieces.

Preheat oven to 400 degrees.

Prepare Béchamel Sauce. Pour Béchamel into an earthenware pot and bring to a simmer over a low heat setting. Gradually add cheese while constantly stirring until melted and well blended into sauce. Add cream and egg yolks and wisk to blend. Season with salt, cayenne, and white pepper. Remove from heat.

Fold in the asparagus tips. Transfer to a casserole dish, sprinkle the top with bread crumb/Parmesan mixture, then dot with clarified butter. Place casserole into oven and bake for 15 minutes. *Serves 4.*

RED BEANS AND RICE

Red Beans and Rice is the traditional Monday dish in New Orleans for two important reasons. The first is because Monday used to be washday. While the wash was being done, the beans could simmer for the hours it takes without much attention to the pot.

The other reason is that after the chicken (which was then considered the expensive meal of the week) was served on Sunday, the family budget generally called for a balance of expenditures. Red Beans is as economical as it is delicious.

1 lb. red kidney beans, in
    enough water to cover
2 qt. water
½ lb. salted pork or ham hocks
1 yellow onion, diced
2 cloves garlic, minced
1 sprig celery, finely chopped
½ tsp. salt

½ tsp. white pepper
⅛ tsp. thyme
1 bay leaf
½ cup of water
6 links smoked sausage
1 tsp. finely chopped parsley
1 tbsp. softened butter
5-6 cups cooked rice

Rinse and soak beans in enough water to cover overnight. Drain the beans and fill a medium-sized pot with 2 qt. of water. Add pork meat or ham hocks. Bring to a slow boil then add beans, onions, garlic, and celery. Season with salt, pepper, thyme, and bay leaf. Allow to slow boil for 2 hours stirring occasionally.

In a medium-sized skillet, fry the smoked sausage in ½ cup water until browned on all sides. Remove.

Add parsley to beans. Remove from heat then swirl in softened butter until well blended. Serve beans over a bed of rice and add a link of smoked sausage to each serving plate. *Serves 6.*

French bread and Barq's root beer—a must!

STEWED SNAP BEANS WITH POTATOES

Snap beans with potatoes have been a favorite of mine since I was a child. It is still served up in my kitchen whenever possible.

2 lb. fresh snap beans
Enough water to cover
1 tsp. salt
2 tbsp. cooking oil
1 small yellow onion, chopped
½ lb. salted pork meat, cubed

2 tomatoes, cubed
1 tsp. black pepper
4 cloves minced garlic
2 potatoes, peeled and cubed
4 cups cooked rice

Rinse snap beans. Snip off the ends and then snap in half. Place the beans in a stew pot and fill with enough water to cover. Add salt to the water and bring to a boil over a medium-high heat setting.

During this time, heat the oil in a heavy skillet. Add the onions and sauté until translucent. Add the salted pork meat and tomatoes, and season with pepper and garlic. Adjust heat to simmer slowly for 10 minutes.

Drain off excess oil then add above mixture to the beans. Add cubed potatoes and allow to slowly boil for about an hour. Adjust seasonings to taste and serve over rice. *Serves 4.*

CAULIFLOWER AU GRATIN

Au gratin dishes have always been popular in New Orleans, cauliflower and potatoes being the most commonly served. The term *au gratin* comes from the fact that the dish is put under the broiler or in an oven to crust the top.

2 cups Béchamel Sauce
2 cups grated cheddar cheese
½ cup half & half cream
2 egg yolks
Salt to taste
Pinch cayenne pepper
⅛ tsp. white pepper

1 head cauliflower, boiled and
**   cut into bite-sized pieces**
Mixture of 2 tbsp. fine bread
**   crumbs and 1 tbsp. grated**
**   Parmesan cheese**
2 tbsp. clarified butter
1 tbsp. finely chopped parsley

Preheat oven to 400 degrees.
Prepare Béchamel Sauce.
Pour Béchamel into an earthenware pot and bring to a simmer over a low heat setting. Add cheddar cheese and stir until melted and well blended into the sauce. Add the cream and egg yolks and whisk until well blended. Season with salt, cayenne, and white pepper. Remove from heat.

In a large, oven-proof casserole dish, pour half of the sauce to cover the bottom. Arrange the cauliflower pieces on top then pour the remaining sauce over the cauliflower.

Sprinkle the bread crumb/Parmesan mixture over the casserole, dot with clarified butter, and bake for 15 minutes. Garnish with a sprinkle of parsley. *Serves 4-6.*

EGGPLANT JEAN-LUC

This dish I named after famed chef and friend Jean-Luc Albin. It exemplifies Creole cookery in its purest form.

ANCHOVY BUTTER

6 anchovies	1 tbsp. chopped parsley
½ cup softened butter	2 cloves minced garlic

Combine above ingredients and mix well with a wooden spoon. Refrigerate for 30 minutes.

1 cup milk	3 large tomatoes
1 egg	Salt to taste
⅔ cup fine bread crumbs	Pepper to taste
⅓ cup finely grated Parmesan cheese	1 cup flour
	4 oz. cooking oil
1 large eggplant	

In a mixing bowl, combine the milk and egg and beat with a wire wisk until well blended.

In a separate bowl, combine the bread crumbs with the grated Parmesan cheese and blend well.

Peel one large eggplant and slice across, forming 6 ½-inch rounds. Cut the ends off of the tomatoes and cut 6 similar ½-inch slices to accommodate the eggplant slices.

Preheat your grill to a medium heat setting. Season the tomato slices with salt and pepper and place on the grill. Cook for about 3 minutes on each side.

On a baking sheet, lightly flour the eggplant slices, pass each through the milk/egg wash, then coat evenly with the bread crumb mixture.

Heat the cooking oil to about 375 degrees, then fry the eggplant slices on both sides until golden brown. Remove the eggplant rounds from the skillet and place on a dry cloth to rid of excess oil. Center on serving plates and top each with a tomato slice and garnish with a crown of Anchovy Butter. *Serves 6.*

FRENCH FRIED EGGPLANT JULIENNE

It was about 1766 when the Spanish brought the eggplant to the colony of New Orleans. It was soon afterward that the entire population became enamored with its remarkable variable qualities. Stuffed, fried, smothered, julienned, the eggplant has appropriated an important chair in the seating of principal vegetables and vegetable dishes of Big Easy cuisine.

This unusual preparation—the powdered sugar makes it so—is one that came from the neighboring sugarcane plantations. It has been a popular family recipe at our restaurant for more than three-quarters of a century.

1 large eggplant	**2 cups milk**
2 cups cooking oil	**1½ cups bread crumbs**
1 cup flour	**½ cup powdered sugar**
2 eggs	

Cup the ends off one large eggplant and trim off the outer skin. Hold it on one end and slice downward to achieve ¼-inch lengthwise slices. One eggplant should yield about 7 slices. Cut each of these slices into ¼-inch julienne strips.

Heat the cooking oil in a deep-well frying pan to 375 degrees.

In a mixing bowl, add the flour and dredge the julienned eggplant strips to cover completely and evenly. In a separate bowl beat the eggs using a wire whisk into the milk. Coat the eggplant strips well in this batter. Remove to another bowl containing the bread crumbs, dredge on all sides, and place the strips into the hot oil. Fry for about 1 minute on each side or until golden brown.

Remove to folded paper towels to drain. Place the hot eggplant strips on a serving platter and sprinkle with powdered sugar. *Serves 6.*

JAMBALAYA

This is a dish that is extremely popular and most illustrative of the Spanish influence on Creole cookery. It is from Paella that the Jambalaya dish is derived, while it has become a very Louisiana preparation.

Like gumbo, Jambalaya can be made with any number or variance of ingredients. This "mixed" recipe, which includes ham, chicken, and shrimp, produces a rounded-out flavor that is very appealing.

½ cup olive oil
2 medium yellow onions, chopped
2 ribs celery, finely diced
½ green bell pepper, finely chopped
1 15-oz. can tomatoes, chopped
2 tbsp. tomato paste
4 cloves garlic, minced
¼ tsp. white pepper

⅛ tsp. cayenne pepper
¼ tsp. ground thyme
Salt to taste
½ lb. diced ham
½ lb. chicken breast, boiled and cubed
2 lb. shrimp, boiled, peeled, and chopped
4 cups cooked rice
½ cup finely chopped parsley

In a large pan, sauté in olive oil the onions, celery, and bell pepper until tender, about 5 minutes. Add the tomatoes, tomato paste, and garlic. Season with white pepper, cayenne pepper, and thyme; salt to taste. Allow to slowly simmer over a low heat setting for 15 minutes. Stir in the ham, chicken, and shrimp and allow to cook for 5 minutes.

Add the rice and parsley and stir while cooking for 10 more minutes. *Serves 8.*

STUFFED MIRLITON
WITH LOBSTER BITS

Like eggplant, we stuff mirliton with any number of garnishes. Aside from the more usual ingredients such as crabmeat and shrimp, this recipe employs lobster, which in a way raises the dish to a status of haute cuisine that can be enjoyed as a more particular delicacy.

4 1-lb. lobsters
Enough Fish Stock or water for
  boiling
4 mirlitons
Enough water to cover
½ cup clarified butter (reserve 1
  tbsp. for baking)
½ cup diced ham
1 small onion, diced fine
2 cloves minced garlic

½ tsp. ground thyme
1 tbsp. finely chopped parsley
  (reserve 1 tsp. for garnish)
Salt to taste
Pepper to taste
1 tbsp. fine bread crumbs
  mixed with 1 tsp. grated
  Parmesan cheese
1 tbsp. pimento strips
Parsley for garnish

Preheat oven to 375 degrees.

Boil lobsters in Fish Stock or water in a rolling boil for 15 minutes. Cut in half lengthwise and remove meat from tails and claws. Chop in small pieces and hold aside.

In a medium pot filled with enough water to cover the mirlitons, blanch for 5 minutes. Remove and allow to cool enough to handle. Half each mirliton and scoop out each pulp, keeping shells in tact.

Mash pulp and sauté in clarified butter for 3 minutes. Add lobster bits, ham, onion, garlic, thyme, and parsley. Simmer for 10 minutes while constantly stirring. Season with salt and pepper. Stir and cook for an additional 5 minutes.

Fill the mirliton shells with the stuffing mixture. Top with a sprinkle of bread crumb and Parmesan cheese mixture and dot with the reserved clarified butter.

Place stuffed mirlitons onto a baking sheet and then into the oven to bake for 20 minutes at 375 degrees or until browned. Garnish with pimento strips and parsley. *Serves 8.*

FRIED ONIONS RINGS

One of the nice things about Galatoire's is that we serve not only the classic Creole dishes that have made New Orleans famous for its food, but we also serve the simple things that so many people love to enjoy.

1 cup milk	**⅛ tsp. cayenne pepper**
1 egg	**1 large yellow onion**
1 tsp. salt	**1 cup flour**
¼ tsp. black pepper	**Oil for frying**

In a bowl, beat the milk together with the egg, salt, black pepper, and cayenne.

Slice the onion into ½-inch thick rounds. Dip them in the egg wash, dredge in the flour, dip into the egg wash a second time, and again dredge in the flour.

Deep fry at approximately 375 degrees until golden brown. Drain on absorbent paper and serve. *Makes 2 servings.*

PETITS POIS PEAS A LA FRANCAISE

A truly classical French dish, the ham, mushrooms, and lettuce make this vegetable dish something special. *Petit pois* means "small peas," and the dish is far better if young peas are used rather than mature larger peas.

There is a sweetness to their taste and a delicacy of texture that adds measurably to the preparation.

1 cup diced ham
1 cup sliced mushrooms
2 cups shredded lettuce
4 tbsp. clarified butter
Generous pinch of white
   pepper

Salt to taste
1 cup water or light stock
2 cups petit pois peas
1 tbsp. kneaded butter (equal
   portions of flour and softened butter)

In a large saucepan, sauté the diced ham, mushrooms, and shredded lettuce in the clarified butter until the lettuce is limp. Season with a generous pinch of white pepper and salt to taste. Add the water or stock and simmer for 2-3 minutes. Add the peas and fold into mixture. Heat, then add the kneaded butter. This will thicken the mixture to the desired consistency. *Serves 4.*

Note: You may want to adjust the consistency if too thick by simply adding a little water or stock. When hot, serve in a casserole dish.

POTATOES BRABANT

I am still amazed at how a preparation such as this raises the simple potato to a thing of far greater deliciousness. It is easy to prepare and can complement almost any entrée.

4 Idaho potatoes
1 cup vegetable oil
¼ cup clarified butter

2 cloves garlic, minced
Salt to taste
1 tsp. finely chopped parsley

Peel and rinse the potatoes, cut each in half lengthwise, then across into small cubes. Heat the vegetable oil in a large skillet over a medium heat setting. Deep fry the potato cubes while turning until golden brown. Transfer to a dry cloth and set aside.

In a separate pan, sauté the garlic in the butter over a low heat setting, seasoning with salt, for 2 minutes. Add parsley and pour over potatoes. *Serves 6.*

POTATOES AU GRATIN

Au gratin means to create a gratin or crust on the top of the preparation. Potatoes and cauliflower are our most common *au gratin* offerings, but I have also included an Asparagus au Gratin in this collection of recipes.

4 Idaho potatoes, boiled and coarsely chopped
2 cups Béchamel Sauce
1 cup half & half cream
2 cups grated cheddar cheese
Salt to taste

¼ tbsp. white pepper
2 tbsp. fine bread crumbs mixed with 1 tbsp. grated Parmesan cheese
½ cup clarified butter
1 tbsp. finely chopped parsley

Preheat broiler.
Prepare Béchamel Sauce.
In a medium pot, add cream and grated cheddar cheese. Slowly simmer over a medium-low heat setting while stirring until cheese is melted and well blended into Béchamel Sauce. Fold in potatoes, season with salt and pepper. Spoon potato mixture into a large casserole dish then top with bread crumb and Parmesan cheese mixture. Dot with clarified butter, then place into the oven to brown top. Garnish with parsley. *Serves 4-6.*

FRENCH FRIED POTATOES

These are fairly large potato slices for fried potatoes—a welcome departure from the fare found most often these days.

In years past one of New Orleans' most popular meals with the market folk was potato po' boys. These days, though, people prefer them as a side course to better fare.

2 large ripe Idaho potatoes
Oil for frying, heated

Salt

Peel the potatoes and cut into eight wedges. Wash and pat the wedges dry and add them to the hot oil.

Cook for approximately 7 minutes, or until golden brown on all sides. Drain on absorbent paper, salt lightly, and serve. *Makes 2 servings.*

HASHED BROWN POTATOES

Even in Creole cookery there is place for hashed brown potatoes. It is not an uncommon request to come to the kitchen at Galatoire's. The way I prepare them is simple and apparently well received by the number of individuals who order them.

1 boiled potato, peeled   **1 tbsp. clarified butter**
Pinch salt   **2 sprigs finely chopped parsley**
Pinch white pepper

Dice potato and season with salt and pepper.

Heat butter in a small sauté pan. Spoon in potatoes to the mold of the pan and fry over a moderate heat setting for about 4 minutes. If possible, flip-toss to cook the other side or turn over into another sauté pan to keep potatoes intact. Cook for another few minutes until golden brown. Transfer to a plate and garnish with a sprinkle of parsley. *Serves 1.*

Simply repeat for more.

POTATOES LYONNAISE

Many of the early merchants, those who sold the meat and produce in the French Market of New Orleans Vieux Carré, were of Lyon-French extraction. These bold pioneers who came to this morass of land were the backbone of the community.

The famous cuisine of Lyon, one of France's most revered cuisines, was incorporated into the Creole pot. This simple potato dish, however, underwent few changes. Its simplicity is its essence.

4 medium potatoes
Enough salted water to cover
2 medium yellow onions
½ cup clarified butter

Salt to taste
White pepper to taste
1 tsp. finely chopped parsley

Place potatoes in a pot filled with salted water to cover. Boil for 25 minutes. Drain into a collander and allow to cool. Peel potatoes using a butter knife. Slice each potato in half lengthwise, then slice each half across into thin semicircular slices.

Peel and cut the ends from each onion. Place on flat ends and cut in half. Then cut the halves into julienne slices.

In a large sauté pan, heat 4 tbsp. of the clarified butter on a medium setting and sauté onions until transluscent. Remove and drain off excess butter. Put aside.

In a separate sauté pan, heat remaining butter on a medium heat setting and sauté the potato slices until they are light brown. Salt and pepper to taste.

Fold in the onions and continue to sauté the combination for 2 minutes. Remove onto serving plates. Garnish with a sprinkle of parsley. *Serves 4.*

Note: This recipe is also included in Salads as Warm Potato Salad Lyonnaise.

GRILLED POTATO WEDGES

Potatoes, in their infinite variety of preparations, remain one of the most popular starches that exists. Another simple example here is the Grilled Potato Wedges that can be served with any entrée to round out the dinner.

2 large Idaho potatoes
1 tbsp. oil mixed with 1 clove
  minced garlic

1 tsp. finely chopped parsley
1 tsp. clarified butter

Preheat the grill.

Peel the potatoes then cut in half lengthwise. Slice across diagonally into $\frac{1}{8}$-inch slices. Coat each slice with the oil and garlic mixture. Grill on each side for about 2 minutes, until well marked. Remove and garnish with parsley and brush with clarified butter. *Serves 4.*

NEW ORLEANS DIRTY RICE

It is truly marvelous how the Creoles had the culinary sense to take even the least of products, the chicken livers, and make them into a complete, other dish. With chicken this accompaniment is terrific as well as it is with any other bird or poultry.

¼ lb. chicken livers
1 tbsp. clarified butter
½ cup finely chopped green
   onions

Salt to taste
¼ tsp. white pepper
1 tsp. finely chopped parsley
4 cups cooked rice

In a medium saucepan, sauté the chicken livers in clarified butter over a medium heat setting until firm. Remove livers from the pan with a slotted spoon. Put aside. Add the green onions to the pan and sauté until tender. Chop the chicken livers and return them to the sauté pan and cook until evenly browned. Add the salt and pepper and stir using a wooden spoon. Add the parsley and rice and turn with a fork until all is well blended. Serve immediately. *Serves 4-6.*

CREAMED SPINACH

This rich spinach dish is one of our most popular vegetable choices. There is a marked elegance to its smooth texture and subtle flavor.

It is also often used as a base for Florentine dishes such as Trout Florentine or Eggs Florentine.

3 cups fresh cooked spinach
1 cup Béchamel Sauce
Salt to taste

⅛ tsp. white pepper
1 chopped hard-boiled egg

Prepare Béchamel Sauce.

In a large saucepan, fold spinach into Béchamel Sauce over a medium-low heat setting. Add salt and pepper. Simmer for 15 minutes, stirring with a wooden spoon. Add chopped hard-boiled egg, then stir.

Remove and keep warm until ready to serve. *Serves 4-6.*

TOMATOES FLORENTINE

Florentine dishes, dishes that employ spinach or creamed spinach in their preparation, are quite popular here. Whether it be fish, eggs, or oysters florentine, the dish is generally quite good.

This tomato offering, and we have the best tomatoes available in our Creole tomatoes, can be served as a vegetable with almost any entrée. Sometimes I have them alone for a light lunch or late supper.

1 small yellow onion, chopped	4 medium tomatoes
¼ cup clarified butter	2 tbsp. bacon bits
2 cups Creamed Spinach	2 tbsp. grated Parmesan cheese
Salt to taste	1 tbsp. chopped parsley
⅛ tsp. white pepper	

Preheat oven to 350 degrees.

Sauté onion using half of the clarified butter (2 tbsp.) over a low heat setting until tender. Add Creamed Spinach and season with salt and pepper. Simmer to heat.

Cut the tops off the tomatoes and a thin slice from the bottoms. Carefully scoop out most of the pulp, keeping the shell and bottoms in tact. Fill the cavities with Creamed Spinach. Top with a sprinkle of bacon followed by the same of Parmesan cheese. Dot the tomatoes with the remaining clarified butter and bake for 20-25 minutes at 350 degrees. Garnish with a sprinkle of parsley. *Serves 4.*

FRIED TOMATOES

Tomatoes are equally as well enjoyed by our customers as are fried onions and eggplant.

It is important to use tomatoes that are not too ripe—not, say, as ripe as you would want for a salad—so that they don't collapse in the frying process and still have a relatively firm texture after cooking.

1 cup milk	2 large slightly unripe
1 egg	tomatoes
1 tsp. salt	1 cup flour
¼ tsp. black pepper	Oil for frying
⅛ tsp. cayenne pepper	

In a bowl, beat the milk together with the egg, salt, black pepper, and cayenne.

Slice the tomato into ½-inch thick rounds. Dip them in the egg wash, dredge in the flour, dip into the egg wash a second time, and again dredge in the flour.

Deep fry at approximately 375 degrees until golden brown. Drain on absorbent paper and serve. *Makes 2 servings.*

GRILLED TOMATOES PARMESAN WITH ANCHOVY FILETS

The tomato was another of the vegetables that the Spanish added to the Creole kitchen. Although it was indigenous to Central and South America, it was not until the Spanish brought it home to Spain in the 1560s that Europe first began using it in their cuisines. Originally it was brought as an ornamental plant, the fruit of which was believed to be poisonous.

Fortunately, some brave soul eventually ate the fruit and opened the door to the development of endless varieties of dishes now made internationally with tomatoes. This simple dish is easy and good. It makes a superb vegetable accompaniment to almost any entrée.

4 large tomatoes	**16 anchovy filets**
1 tsp. salt	**½ cup grated Parmesan cheese**
½ tsp. freshly ground black pepper	**1 tbsp. minced parsley**

Heat the grill to a medium heat.

Slice the ends off each tomato, then halve them. Season with salt and pepper.

Place all 8 tomato slices on the grill and to cook for about 3 minutes on each side. Cross 2 anchovies over each tomato slice then sprinkle on the Parmesan cheese. Place under a broiler flame for 2 minutes to melt the Parmesan.

Garnish with minced parsley. Serve 2 slices per person. *Serves 4.*

Eggs and Omelettes

EGGS BENEDICT

One of the most renowned, as well as popular, offerings in the egg category is Eggs Benedict.

In years past, eggs were very popular in New Orleans as evening and late night, or after theater, "soupers."

During carnival season, Eggs Benedict are often served as supper after the balls. But most popular, are Eggs Benedict served as part of the all-popular New Orleans brunch, that marvelous invention that ties together breakfast and lunch into one very scrumptious and often lavish meal.

2 cups Hollandaise Sauce	**8 slices Canadian bacon**
8 English muffins, split	**8 eggs, poached**
2 tbsp. clarified butter	**8 truffle slices**

Prepare Hollandaise Sauce and set aside.

Toast English muffins, faces up, and place on serving plates, keeping warm.

Sauté Canadian bacon slices in the clarified butter for 2 minutes. Place one slice on each muffin. Poach the eggs and place one atop each muffin.

Top with equal portions of Hollandaise and place a sliver of truffle on each. *Serves 4.*

POACHED EGGS A LA CREOLE

All of the original land-grant holders, those who were within the city limits, had a sufficient-sized lot to hold a home and a yard for raising vegetables and poultry, as well as occasional cow. Since raising poultry was an essential part of these little farms, the business of the egg was a serious one.

Many, many egg dishes exist in Creole cooking. This particular recipe calls for the essential sauce—Creole Sauce.

2 cups Creole Sauce	4 English muffins, split
8 slices Canadian bacon	8 eggs, poached
1 tbsp. clarified butter	

Prepare Creole Sauce.

Sauté bacon slices in a medium pan in clarified butter until hot. Transfer to paper towels. Toast English muffins. Place a slice of bacon onto each muffin then place a poached egg on each. Top with Creole Sauce and serve. *Serves 4.*

EGGS ROY AU FOIE GRAS

One of my best friends and fellow restaurateurs is Roy Guste. He inspired me to begin this book and pushed me to finish it. An experienced author himself and the recognized authority on Creole cuisine—I dedicate this extravagant recipe to him.

2 tbsp. softened butter	2 English muffins (4 halves),
2 apples, peeled, cored, and	cut into wedges
sliced into eighths	1 tbsp. apple jelly
¼ cup raisins	4 eggs
⅛ tsp. cinnamon	½ oz. duck pâté

In a heavy saucepan, melt the butter and add apple slices and raisins, and sauté for 2 minutes or until tender. Add cinnamon and hold aside.

Toast the muffins on both sides. Spread with apple jelly and hold aside.

In a medium sauté pan, fry the eggs and place one onto each serving plate. In the same pan, braise the slices of pâté for about 30 seconds minute on each side.

Place 1 slice of pâté onto each egg. Garnish with a wedge of jellied muffin. Then spoon equal portions of apple and raisin sauce on the opposite side of each plate. *Serves 4.*

EGGS SARDOU

The French playwright Victorien Sardou was fêted in the city during a visit here to mount a production of several of his plays in the French Opera House.

A popular chef at the time, knowing of Sardou's love for artichokes, served him this invention. Sardou was so delighted by the recipe that the chef named it after him. Soon all of the major restaurants in the city had placed it on their menus.

This preparation can also be made with cooked crabmeat or shrimp.

1 cup Hollandaise Sauce	**2 tsp. vinegar**
8 artichokes	**8 eggs**
Enough water to cover	**1 cup Creamed Spinach**
4 cups water	**2 pinches paprika**

Prepare the Hollandaise Sauce.

Place artichokes into a medium-sized pot filled with enough water to cover. Put a lid on the pot and boil for 30 minutes over a medium heat setting. Remove and allow to cool. Peel the leaves from the artichokes. *Note:* You may want to save the leaves for other use. Remove artichoke bottom and using a spoon, remove and discard choke. Slice off remaining stem from bottoms.

In a medium saucepan, bring 4 cups of water to a boil, add vinegar, and poach eggs for 3 minutes. Turn off heat.

Spoon equal portions of Creamed Spinach onto each of 4 plates, then artichoke bottoms. Using a slotted spoon, carefully remove eggs from the water and transfer 2 onto each bottom. Top with a spoonful of Hollandaise Sauce. Garnish with a light sprinkle of paprika. *Serves 4.*

EGGS SUZETTE

It is the relationship of the orange and brandy to flavor the sauce for this egg dish that brings forth the name Suzette, as in the famous sweet crêpe dessert of the same appellation.

Suzette was herself a member of La Comédie-Française, and in 1837 in Paris, she found herself playing the part of a chambermaid in a theatrical production in which she served crepes as part of the play. The Restaurant Marivaux, which was responsible for the preparation of the crepes, invented the crepe recipe and named it after the actress.

1 orange, reserve juice and 1 slice for garnish	2 cups water
1 lemon	Dash white wine vinegar or lemon juice
1 tbsp. lemon juice	1 oz. brandy
4 tbsp. softened butter	4 eggs
2 tbsp. powdered sugar	2 English muffins, split

Peel zest of orange and lemon using a potato peeler. Slice the peelings into fine strips. In a saucepan, combine the softened butter along with the orange and lemon zest strips, the juice of one orange and 1 tbsp. lemon juice. Add the powdered sugar and stir the mixture over low heat gently for about 10 minutes until sauce begins to take on a smooth, thick consistency.

During this time, fill an egg poacher or saucepan with 2 cups water and heat to a boil. Add the dash of wine vinegar or lemon juice.

Sauce Suzette may be introduced as a flambé, usually done for effect. If you elect to present as such, heat the brandy in a shot glass and half-submerge in the pan containing water to be used before poaching eggs. One minute will be appropriate. Remove brandy and add to Suzette sauce. Tip top end of pan so a small amount of brandy comes in contact with the flame, or implement a lighter. Brandy is highly flammable so mind your use.

When flame is achieved, agitate pan until flame expires and alcohol is burned off. Remove sauce from fire.

Poach the eggs for no more than 4 minutes, during which time, toast the halved English muffins. Remove the eggs using a slotted spoon.

Place an egg atop each halved muffin. Top with Suzette sauce and garnish with one halved orange slice dividing each egg. *Serves 2.*

ASPARAGUS OMELETTE

Asparagus is not a common filling for an omelette, which is what makes it a delightful alternative to other omelettes.

3 eggs	**1 tbsp. softened butter**
Salt to taste	**3 blanched asparagus tips**
Pepper to taste	

In a mixing bowl, break the eggs and season with salt and pepper. Beat with a fork only long enough to blend thoroughly.

In an omelette pan or treated aluminum pan, heat the softened butter. As it melts, swirl it around to film surface and sides. Using a fork in one hand, stir the eggs quickly over the bottom of the pan. Spoon the chopped blanched asparagus tips into the center of the omelette. Tilt the pan so that the omelette rolls toward the far lip of the pan and out onto the center of a serving plate.

Slice the asparagus garnish in half lengthwise and lay on top of the omelette. Serve. *Makes 1 omelette.*

BACON AND MUSHROOM OMELETTE

Bacon seems as natural a garnish to an omelette as almost anything can be. The fresh mushrooms add the dimension of taste and texture that becomes something special.

3 eggs	3 strips of bacon, fried crisp
1 tbsp. softened butter	and chopped
Salt to taste	½ cup fresh mushrooms,
Pepper to taste	sautéed in 1 tbsp. butter

In a mixing bowl, break the eggs and season with salt and pepper. Beat with a fork only long enough to blend thoroughly.

In an omelette pan or treated aluminum pan, heat the softened butter. As it melts, swirl it around to film surface and sides. Using a fork in one hand, stir the eggs quickly over the bottom of the pan. Add the chopped bacon and sautéed mushrooms to the center of the omelette before folding. Place on a hot plate and serve. *Makes 1 omelette.*

CRABMEAT OMELETTE

Crabmeat, when we have it, seems to find it way into every preparation that we have in New Orleans cookery. Its freshness is extremely important since it will carry the flavor of the omelette practically on its own.

1 tbsp. butter	Salt to taste
1 tbsp. finely chopped green	Pepper to taste
onion	¼ lb. crabmeat
3 eggs, lightly beaten	1 tsp. chopped parsley

In the omelette pan, heat the butter and sauté the chopped green onions until limp. Add the eggs and salt and pepper. Add the crabmeat and just bring to a hot temperature. Pour in the beaten eggs and, using a fork, stir the mixture quickly over the bottom of the pan. Fold into thirds when cooked.

Garnish with chopped parsley. *Makes 1 omelette.*

CRAWFISH ÉTOUFFÉE OMELETTE

Crawfish Étouffée is not only a delicious dish on its own, but as garnish to an omelette it can become even more special. It's also a grand way to finish off the last ladle in the pot.

In devising interesting omelette variations, I use whatever I have at hand. Sometimes I use leftover red beans, or white beans, other times I use the remainder of stuffed eggplant or even gumbo that I thicken and use as a sauce. Variations are an important key to Creole cooking.

3 eggs	**1 tbsp. softened butter**
Salt to taste	**½ cup Crawfish Étouffée**
Pepper to taste	**1 tsp. chopped parsley**

In a mixing bowl, break the eggs and season with salt and pepper. Beat with a fork only long enough to blend thoroughly.

In an omelette pan or treated aluminum pan, heat the softened butter. As it melts, swirl it around to film surface and sides. Using a fork in one hand, stir the eggs quickly over the bottom of the pan. Spoon the Crawfish Étouffée onto the center of the omelette. Tilt the pan so that the omelette rolls toward the far lip of the pan and out onto the center of a serving plate.

Garnish with chopped parsley and serve. *Makes 1 omelette.*

CREOLE OMELETTE

Since Creole Sauce is perhaps the most important of all sauces in our cooking, it can appear almost anywhere—and it does. Here as sauce to an omelette, there with shrimp or chicken. It is essential and most indicative of the fusion of French and Spanish cuisines that are the base of Creole.

1 cup Creole Sauce, heated
3 large eggs
Salt to taste

Pepper to taste
1 tbsp. softened butter

Prepare the Creole Sauce, adjusting the ingredients for a 1-cup recipe or complete recipe as outlined and reserve remaining amount.

In a mixing bowl, break the eggs and season with salt and pepper. Beat with a fork only long enough to blend thoroughly.

In an omelette pan or treated aluminum pan, heat the softened butter. As it melts, swirl it around to film surface and sides. Using a fork in one hand, stir the eggs quickly over the bottom of the pan. Quickly spoon 2 tbsp. of the hot Creole Sauce towards the near end of the pan. Tilt the pan so that the omelette rolls toward the far lip of the pan onto the center of the serving plate.

Garnish or top with equal amounts of the Creole Sauce.

Wipe the pan clean with a dry cloth and repeat the process for additional omelettes. *Makes 1 omelette.*

HAM AND CHEESE OMELETTE

Even the standard "diner" recipes must be kept handy for those who insist on having them. It is nice in this recipe to allow the butter to just barely begin to color to give the omelette that familiar nutty taste.

1 tbsp. butter
3 eggs, lightly beaten
1 tbsp. finely chopped ham
1 tbsp. grated American cheese

Salt to taste
Pepper to taste
1 tsp. chopped parsley

In the omelette pan, heat the butter and pour in the lightly beaten eggs. Season with salt and pepper. Using a fork, quickly stir the eggs over the bottom of the pan and add the chopped ham and grated cheese before folding the omelette into thirds.

Turn out onto a heated dinner plate, garnish with chopped parsley, and serve. *Makes 1 omelette.*

OYSTER OMELETTE

Oysters, as with crabmeat, seem to find their way into every preparation that we have in New Orleans cookery. Since the oysters are poached before adding them to the omelette, this is a dish that can be served any time of the year ... not just the R months as once was the rule.

1 tbsp. butter	3 eggs, lightly beaten
1 tbsp. finely chopped green onions	Salt to taste
	Pepper to taste
4 oysters, poached lightly until their edges curl	1 tsp. chopped parsley

In the omelette pan, heat the butter and sauté the chopped green onions until limp. Add the oysters and just bring to a hot temperature. Pour in the beaten eggs, stir quickly with a fork, season to taste with salt and pepper, and fold into thirds when cooked.

Garnish with chopped parsley. *Makes 1 omelette.*

SHRIMP OMELETTE

Shrimp, oysters, and crabmeat are often used in similar preparations. No exception here. The marvelous thing about an omelette is that any garnish or filling can be used.

1 tbsp. butter	Salt to taste
1 tbsp. finely chopped green onions	Pepper to taste
	1 tsp. chopped parsley
3 eggs, lightly beaten	
4 medium-sized boiled shrimp, peeled	

In the omelette pan, heat the butter and sauté the chopped green onions until limp. Add the shrimp and just bring to a hot temperature. Pour in the beaten eggs, stir quickly with a fork, season to taste with the salt and pepper, and fold into thirds when cooked.

Garnish with chopped parsley. *Makes 1 omelette.*

Sauces

BEARNAISE SAUCE

It was the renowned French chef Collinet who invented this sauce and named it after the birthplace of King Henri IV—Béarn. Henri IV was the first king of France who was a serious proponent of the culinary arts.

Béarnaise can also be used as the starting base for many other sauces such as Choron, Foyot, Arlesienne, and Valois.

1 cup Béchamel Sauce	⅓ cup tarragon vinegar
1 cup Hollandaise Sauce	Salt to taste
2 tbsp. chopped green onions	2 pinches white pepper
1 tsp. tarragon leaves, dried	Pinch cayenne pepper
and chopped	1 tsp. chopped parsley

Prepare Béchamel and Hollandaise sauces and hold aside.

In a large saucepan, simmer green onions and tarragon leaves in vinegar over a low heat setting until vinegar evaporates. Add Béchamel Sauce and blend with a wire whisk. Add salt, white pepper, and cayenne pepper, then simmer for 2 minutes. Add parsley.

Remove from heat and gradually fold in Hollandaise Sauce using a wooden spoon until well blended.

Note: Sauce will usually hold well heated in a bain-marie, but best to add Hollandaise to heated Béchamel Sauce just prior to serving. *Makes 2 cups.*

BECHAMEL SAUCE

The most basic of the three major French sauce groups, the others being Velouté and Demi-glas, this preparation is often called upon to uplift even the most mundane of dishes.

The Marquis de Bechameil, for whom the sauce is named, received the honor from the chef of Louis XIV, for whom Bechamiel served as majordomo, after his tenure as steward to, and appropriately enough, the Duc d'Orleans.

4 cups milk	½ cup white wine
½ tsp. salt	½ cup butter
½ tsp. white pepper	½ cup flour
Pinch cayenne pepper	1 cup heavy cream, reserved (if
1 bay leaf	needed)

In a small pot, heat the milk to a simmer. Reduce heat and add salt, pepper, cayenne, bay leaf, and white wine. Simmer for a few minutes.

In a separate pot, melt the butter on a low heat setting and add the flour, constantly stirring the roux with a wire whisk.

Strain the milk through a fine sieve and pour it into the roux pot, stirring constantly in a circular motion. The sauce will thicken.

Add heavy cream, if needed, to enrich the sauce or to thin it out if it becomes too thick.

Allow to simmer for about 5 minutes to cook the flour taste out.
Makes 4 cups.

BORDELAISE SAUCE

Inspired by a wealth of the world's greatest wines, the chefs of Bordeaux, a province of France, created this sauce to complement the food of their area. When émigrés from Bordeaux settled in Louisiana, they naturally brought their best recipes.

Many of these émigrés arrived during the second wave of French settlement in Louisiana, which occurred during the French Revolution. These were the aristocrats who came to escape the ravages of the Reign of Terror, and the guillotine.

2 finely chopped shallots	4 oz. beef bone marrow, boiled
2 cloves minced garlic	for 2 minutes
1 cup red wine	1 oz. brandy
Salt to taste	1 tbsp. fincly chopped parsley
Pepper to taste	2 tbsp. or 4 chips solid
1 cup Espagnole Sauce	butter

Combine shallots, minced garlic, and red wine into a saucepan. Boil until reduced by two-thirds. Add salt and pepper, then pour in one cup of Espagnole Sauce. Stir using a wire whisk.

When sauce comes to a boil, add bone marrow that has been boiled and drained. Add brandy and stir. Add parsley. Remove from heat and then add chips of solid butter and swirl in. This will enrich and enhance the sauce. *Makes 1½ cups.*

Note: This sauce complements most grilled meats, beef roasts, and goes particularly well with calf's liver.

COCKTAIL SAUCE

This simple sauce is used for all our boiled seafood. Each cook will, of course, make the recipe to meet his own tastes.

¾ cup ketchup	1 tsp. lemon juice
Dash Worcestershire sauce	1 tbsp. horseradish
Dash Tabasco sauce	⅛ tsp. salt

Combine all ingredients, mix well, and serve chilled. *Makes 1 cup.*

CREOLE SAUCE

This sauce is one of the most important and illustrative of Creole cuisine.

The most important cultures that came together in New Orleans to develop our cookery are the Louisiana Indian, Canadian French as well as the Continental French, and the Spanish. It was during the building of this great city of New Orleans that these people created a new cuisine indigenous to this area, a cuisine that was, before New Orleans, nonexistent.

The most celebrated dishes employing Creole Sauce are Shrimp and Chicken Creole. They are both key entries in our Creole repertoire.

2 cups water	1 bay leaf
2 cups diced onion	2 12-oz. cans whole tomatoes,
2 cups diced celery	crushed
1 cup diced bell pepper	1 12-oz. can tomato puree
4 cloves garlic, minced	4 tbsp. chopped parsley
Salt to taste	½ tsp. sugar
½ tsp. white pepper	1½ tbsp. corn starch
⅛ tsp. ground thyme	

Heat the water to a boil. Add onions, celery, bell pepper, and garlic and season with salt, white pepper, thyme, and bay leaf. Allow vegetables to boil over a medium-high heat setting. Add the tomatoes, tomato puree, parsley, and sugar. Reduce the heat and allow the sauce to simmer 1 hour.

Dilute 2 tbsp. cornstarch in 1 cup of cold water, then gradually pour in a little at a time to achieve your desired thickness. Simmer for 5 minutes more. *Makes 6 cups.*

DEMI-GLACE SAUCE

The Demi-glace is one of the three major sauce bases in classic French Cuisine: Béchamel, Velouté, and Demi-glace.

The Creoles used this classic as a base to heighten their simple cookery onto a level of "Haute-Creole," which lent to the table sophisticated and lavish recipes.

2 cups Espagnole Sauce   1 oz. Madeira wine
2 cups clear Brown Stock   Pinch black pepper
3 large jumbo mushrooms,
   chopped

Combine the Espagnole Sauce, Brown Stock, and chopped mushrooms into a small pot. Allow to simmer on a low heat setting until the sauce has reduced by half. Remove from heat and strain through a fine sieve. Add Madeira wine and pepper for its distinct flavor. *Makes 2 cups.*

Note: This sauce goes beautifully over filet mignon and truly enhances the flavor of any good cut of meat.

ESPAGNOLE SAUCE

The predecessor of this sauce existed long before the tomato was added to the list of ingredients. When the tomato was first brought back from the New World to Europe in the sixteenth century, it was in Spain, Portugal, and Italy where it gained a foothold in popularity.

This French sauce is called Espagnol, or Spanish, because the tomato had gained such acceptance in Spain that its neighbor, France, thought of anything including the tomato as Spanish in origin.

Espagnole Sauce is used as is, or as a base for other sauces.

MIREPOIX

½ yellow onion, finely
   chopped
1 rib of celery, finely chopped
2 carrots, finely diced
¼ lb. bacon, cut into short
   strips and blanched

Pinch ground thyme
Pinch ground bay leaf
Pinch salt
2 tbsp. clarified butter

Prepare a mirepoix by combining diced onion, celery, carrots, and blanched bacon strips, seasoned with finely ground thyme, bay leaf, and salt. In a large saucepan, heat clarified butter and sauté ingredients until tender and lightly browned (approximately 20 minutes), stirring from time to time to prevent sticking. Remove from fire and set aside. *Should make 1 cup of mirepoix.*

¼ cup clarified butter
½ cup flour
3 tbsp. Mirepoix
¼ cup bone marrow, diced

½ cup mushrooms, chopped
2 tomatoes, crushed and peeled
2 qt. Brown Stock

Prepare a brown roux by heating the clarified butter in a large saucepan. Add flour and blend using a wire whisk until achieving a smooth consistency on a low heat setting. Roux should take on a rich brown color. Remove from fire and add 3 tbsp. of Mirepoix, the bone marrow, sliced mushrooms, and crushed, peeled tomatoes. Stir, then add Brown Stock. Stir and place on a low heat setting and allow to simmer for about 2 hours. Stir from time to time to ensure proper or desired consistency. Pour mixture through a fine sieve reserving a smooth, rich, ready sauce. *Makes 2 cups.*

FINANCIERE SAUCE

It is the richness of this sauce that has earned it the title of *Financière*, meaning "the finance minister."

My version here is one that is a minor variation from the old style French-New Orleans classic. It is the chicken livers and olives that make the difference from an already rich sauce Marchand de Vin, to become Financière.

4 cups Marchand de Vin Sauce
4 large chicken livers, minced
8 large green olives, seeded
and sliced

1 tbsp. finely chopped parsley

Prepare Marchand de Vin Sauce and add the chicken livers and green olives. Reduce slightly and add the parsley just before serving.

Serve with chicken, beef, or pork. *Makes 4 cups.*

HOLLANDAISE SAUCE

Hollandaise Sauce is an old favorite of many, and a sauce that can be used with almost any entrée—fish, poultry, or meat. It is the pinch of cayenne that can vary to please any palate.

The sauce is a bit difficult to prepare in that it requires your attention. Too much heat, or too quickly cooked, and it will separate. Hollandaise can also be used as the base of a number of other sauces including Chantilly, Maltaise, Mousseline, or Mikado.

6 egg yolks
2 tbsp. solid butter
Pinch salt
Pinch cayenne pepper

1 tsp. lemon juice
1 tsp. red wine vinegar
2 tbsp. cold water
2 cups clarified butter

In a bain-marie or double boiler, combine the egg yolks with the 2 tbsp. of solid butter cut into small pieces, salt, cayenne pepper, lemon juice, and red wine vinegar. Using a wire whisk, slowly blend the mixture over a medium heat setting allowing the butter to melt into the mixture. Continue to whisk until the mixture takes on a thick, almost coarse, texture.

Remove from the heat and add 2 tbsp. cold water. This will cool the mixture and prevent curdling.

Using a ladle, slowly pour in the clarified butter, whisking the mixture constantly with a circular motion. The sauce should achieve a nice, thick consistency. *Makes 2 cups.*

Note: Do not refrigerate and keep at a constant temperature. Any sudden change in temperature will cause the sauce to separate or break.

MARCHAND DE VIN SAUCE

The "wine merchant's sauce" is what *Marchand de Vin* translates to be. In the old stalls in Les Halles, the old central market in Paris, all the merchants had their breakfasts or lunches going on small coal stoves so that it would be ready when they had time to eat. The wine merchant's pot was often a size larger than the others so that he could share his sauce to be ladled over the others' prepared dishes.

¼ cup clarified butter
2 tbsp. flour
½ cup green onions, finely
   chopped
3 cloves garlic, minced
Salt to taste

⅛ tsp. white pepper
Pinch cayenne pepper
2½ cups beef stock
1 cup red wine
½ cup chopped mushrooms
1 tbsp. parsley, finely chopped

Prepare a dark roux by combining the clarified butter and flour. Continuously stir mixture over a low heat setting until dark brown (about 10 minutes). Add the green onions and garlic to simmer for 2 minutes. Season with salt, white pepper, and cayenne pepper, then pour in beef stock and red wine. Add mushrooms and parsley, then simmer for 20 minutes more. *Makes 2 cups.*

MEUNIERE SAUCE

In the style of the miller's wife is what this sauce recalls. In New Orleans we tend to make the sauce a little more hearty than its timid French cousin.

1 lb. butter
1 tbsp. red wine vinegar

1 tbsp. fresh lemon juice

In a medium, heavy pot, melt the butter over a medium-low heat setting, constantly stirring with a wire whisk until the butter achieves a dark brown tint. Mix equal portions of vinegar and lemon juice and drip small amounts into the butter while vigorously whisking. *Note:* The vinegar mixture will cause the butter to rise and foam quickly so it is important to mind your whisk.

Remove from heat and strain through a fine sieve. Warm and mix well before use. *Makes 2 cups.*

MUSTARD CREAM SAUCE

Mustard, in its many worldwide varieties, is one of the most important seasonings in the world. In this recipe, the tangy flavor of the mustard is richly subdued by the cream. The addition of the fresh lemon juice delivers the bite that makes the sauce both pungent and most appealing.

In this collection I have used Mustard Cream Sauce as an accompaniment to roast pork tenderloin. It can be used with almost any meats or fish. Try it with grilled chicken breast or grilled filet of fish.

1 pt. heavy cream	**1 egg yolk**
2 tbsp. Dijon mustard	**White pepper to taste**
1 tsp. lemon juice	

Heat the heavy cream so as not to boil, but enough to reduce by one-third, at a low heat setting. Add Dijon mustard and blend into the cream using a wire whisk. Add the lemon juice and egg yolk while whisking. Add white pepper to taste and gently simmer for 2 minutes.

The egg yolk will enrich as well as help thicken the sauce. While stirring, the sauce should achieve a nice, smooth consistency. When this result is achieved, remove the sauce from the heat. If the sauce appears a bit too thin, it will thicken as it stands. *Makes 2 cups.*

REMOULADE SAUCE

A good way to judge a restaurant in our city is by the remoulade sauce. It is one of the earliest dishes to have become a standard in the Creole repertoire, and remains a mainstay to this day.

There is a natural marriage that occurs between the crisp piquant bite of the remoulade and the Gulf of Mexico's splendid offerings of shrimp, crabmeat, and oysters.

I use it in this collection on shrimp as well as oysters and crabmeat. They all go well with the sauce.

1 bunch parsley, stems removed	1 cup red wine vinegar
2 ribs celery	1 tsp. Tabasco sauce
2 cloves garlic	1 tsp. Worcestershire sauce
1 tbsp. minced bell pepper	Salt to taste
1 cup Creole mustard	¼ tsp. black pepper
4 tbsp. paprika	Pinch cayenne pepper
2 tbsp. prepared horseradish	1 pt. salad oil

Using a food processor, chop the parsley, celery, garlic, and bell pepper to a coarse puree. Transfer this to a large mixing bowl. Add the mustard, paprika, horseradish, vinegar, Tabasco, Worcestershire, salt, black pepper, and cayenne pepper. Using a wire whisk, beat constantly adding small amounts of oil at a dribble until the sauce achieves a smooth consistency. Cover and transfer to refrigerator to marinate for 24 hours. *Makes 2 cups.*

REMOULADE BLANC

Although New Orleans is famous for its remoulade sauces, this version leans in the direction of the original French version. The principal difference between the two is color and spiciness. This white remoulade, as opposed to the red-orange remoulade most often found here, is also spicy. The Creole mustard and horseradish give it a pungency that sparks the taste.

1 cup mayonnaise
2 tbsp. Creole mustard
4 green onions, finely chopped
2 tsp. finely chopped parsley
1 tbsp. horseradish

Juice of ½ lemon
1 oz. white wine
Pinch white pepper
Pinch cayenne pepper

To prepare, simply combine all of the above ingredients in a mixing bowl. Using a wire whisk, blend well together. Cover and refrigerate. *Makes 1¾ cups.*

Note: White Remoulade Sauce should possess a distinctly tart and aromatic quality. Some brands of horseradish may lack the punch or potency we look for. If by taste it seems a bit flat, lean on the horseradish.

SAUCE ROBERT

This is another example of a recipe that was born in the French culinary tradition, appearing in cookbooks as early as the 1580s, yet grew to its Creole adulthood in New Orleans. The bite from the vinegar and Dijon mustard is essential to the flavor of the sauce, as is the richness of the white wine and Espagnole Sauce as its base—a true New Orleans touch.

Sauce Robert is served with almost all meats, especially white meats and game.

2 tbsp. butter
1 yellow onion, chopped
1 tbsp. flour
1 cup Brown Stock

¾ cup white wine
2 tbsp. white vinegar
½ cup Espagnole Sauce
2 tbsp. Dijon mustard

In a large saucepan, heat the butter until hot but not burned. Add the chopped onion and sauté until golden brown. Sprinkle in flour and blend well, using a wooden spoon. Allow the flour to brown with the onions.

Pour in the Brown Stock, stirring constantly. Allow the mixture to thicken, then pour in white wine and then the vinegar. Simmer the sauce on a medium setting for 10 minutes while stirring. Pour in Espagnole Sauce. Stir using a wire whisk.

Remove from the fire and allow the sauce to settle for a couple of minutes, then add Dijon mustard and blend into sauce. Strain the sauce through a fine sieve. *Makes 1 cup.*

Note: This sauce complements grilled pork loin beautifully.

VELOUTE SAUCE

Velouté Sauce is one of the principal sauces and sauce bases of French cuisine, the others being Béchamel and Demi-glace.

From Velouté, which differs from Béchamel in that it is made with a stock instead of the milk or cream of Béchamel, many, many other sauces are derived such as Poulette, Supreme, Aurore, Cardinal, etc.

VELOUTE FOR FISH AND OTHER SEAFOOD

1 ½ tbsp. softened butter
1 ½ tbsp. flour, sifted
1 cup Fish Stock
1 tbsp. white wine

1 tbsp. lemon juice
1 egg yolk
1 tsp. finely chopped parsley

VELOUTE FOR POULTRY

Substitute 1 cup chicken stock
    for the Fish Stock

Melt butter in a medium saucepan over a low heat setting. Wisk in the flour to form a roux. When roux is hot, add the stock and whisk constantly. Add the white wine and lemon juice. Mix well, remove from heat, and wisk in the egg yolk and parsley. *Makes 1 cup.*

Note: The Velouté Sauce may be kept warm in a bain-marie until needed. Sauce will thicken if left to cool. If so, add more stock or water to adjust thickness.

Fish and Seafood

COBIA COURT BOUILLON

Cobia, also known as ling or lemon fish, is one of the most prized fish available from off the American Gulf Coast. As a large fish—resembling a shark to a degree—it is more commonly served steaked or in roast cuts.

The court bouillon is a mainstay of Creole cuisine found on the table more commonly served with redfish. I like the court bouillon prepared with this particularly fine fish.

4 cups Fish Stock or Fumet	1 level tsp. salt
1 bell pepper	¼ tsp. cayenne pepper
2 tomatoes	1 tsp. finely minced garlic
1 yellow onion	1 cup dry white wine
4 8-oz. cobia (lemon fish) filets	4 cups cooked rice
2 bay leaves	

Prepare the Fish Fumet (Stock). Allow to cool and put aside.

Slice the bell pepper into thin strips. Peel and dice the tomatoes, halve a yellow onion and cut into thin slices.

In a large saucepan or fish kettle, add the cobia filets, then add bell pepper, tomatoes, onion, and the fish fumet. Season with bay leaves, salt, and cayenne pepper. Add the minced garlic and white wine. On medium-high heat, simmer the mixture for 25 minutes.

Arrange the cooked rice in a circular fashion around the perimeter of each of four serving plates. Place one fish filet in the center of each plate and top with the remaining vegetables and liquid. *Serves 4.*

POMPANO MEUNIERE AMANDINE

Most New Orleanians who move about and dine in the numerous good restaurants in our city will testify to the fact that this is one of our great dishes. The browned butter in the Meunière Sauce and the almonds gild the lily, so to speak, in a way that results in a memorable and often reordered dish.

1 cup Meunière Sauce	¼ tsp. white pepper
4 8-oz. pompano filets	¾ cup toasted almonds, sliced
1 tbsp. vegetable oil	4 sprigs parsley
¼ tsp. paprika	1 lemon, cut into wedges

Prepare the Meunière Sauce and hold aside.
Preheat broiler.
Lightly coat the pompano filets with oil. Season with a dash of paprika and white pepper. Place filets on a large cookie sheet or baking pan skin-side down in a partially closed broiler. Cook for about 12 minutes or until golden brown.
Transfer to serving plates and sprinkle each filet with almonds. Heat and stir Meunière Sauce and ladle each filet with equal portions of sauce. Garnish each plate with a sprig of parsley and a lemon wedge. *Serves 4.*

POMPANO NAPOLEON

There was once an actual plot in New Orleans to capture Napoleon from exile and bring him to New Orleans where he was to live out his life in royal fashion. Hence the Napoleon House Bar & Cafe, which then belonged to the mayor of the city who was going to give the house to Napoleon on his arrival here.

Unfortunately, the details and preparation of the expedition took so long to organize that Napoleon died. In his absence, however, I place this dish before you.

4 8-oz. pompano filets	1 cup heavy cream
8 large jumbo mushrooms	1 tbsp. Dijon mustard
½ cup dry white wine plus 2 tbsp. lemon juice	1 tsp. Creole mustard

Preheat oven to 400 degrees.

Place pompano filets into a large, oven-safe casserole dish. Arrange mushroom buttons in vacant areas of the casserole dish. Moisten the fish filets and mushrooms with the white wine and lemon juice mixture. Cover and place in the heated oven to cook for 12 minutes.

During this time, heat the heavy cream in a large saucepan on a low fire. Add the Dijon and Creole mustards and blend well, using a wire whisk and stirring constantly. Allow to simmer for about 2 minutes, then remove from heat until the fish are done.

Remove the casserole from the oven. Remove the fish from the casserole, reserving the juices.

Pour the juices through a fine sieve, then add to the mustard sauce. Whisk and simmer until you have achieved a nice, smooth sauce.

Spoon a small amount of sauce atop each pompano filet and garnish each plate with two cooked mushroom buttons. *Serves 4.*

GRILLED FILET OF SALMON WITH DILL SAUCE

Although salmon is not a fish indigenous to our local waters, its availability is abundant. Thus, we can truly enjoy this delicate fish as our Cajun forefathers did in Nova Scotia before making their way to Louisiana.

2 cups Velouté Sauce	Salt to taste
1 tsp. fresh dill, chopped	White pepper to taste
4 8-oz. fresh salmon filets	1 lemon, quartered
2 tbsp. vegetable oil	

Prepare Velouté Sauce. Add dill to sauce and slowly simmer over a low heat setting for 2-3 minutes. Keep sauce warm.

Preheat grill or spit to desired temperature. Lightly coat salmon filets with oil and season with salt and pepper. Grill for approximately 3 minutes on each side, allowing for a slightly pink center.

Serve and top with the hot dill sauce. Garnish each filet with a lemon wedge. *Serves 4.*

POACHED FILET OF SALMON HOLLANDAISE

Years ago, salmon was not an unfamiliar fish to this area. Whether they were transported in by boat, or whether they actually were once available in a nearer water then they are now is hard to decipher from old readings. But salmon is definitely here now, and here to stay if the supply permits.

This simple preparation complements the fish, the richness of the Hollandaise somehow matching the richness of the fish itself.

2 cups Hollandaise Sauce
4 8-oz. salmon filets
Enough water to cover
1 yellow onion, thinly sliced
1 sprig fresh thyme
2 bay leaves

Juice of 1 lemon
½ tsp. salt
½ cup white wine
4 sprigs fresh dill
⅛ tsp. paprika

Prepare Hollandaise Sauce and set aside.

In a large saucepan or poacher, fill with enough water to cover salmon. Add onion, thyme, bay leaves, lemon juice, salt, and white wine.

Heat over a medium-low heat setting. When water achieves a slow boil, poach for 5 minutes.

Remove the filets and place them on a clean cloth to drain any excess water.

Place the salmon on serving plates and top with Hollandaise Sauce. Garnish with a small dill leaf and a sprinkle of paprika. *Serves 4.*

RED SNAPPER LOUIS

It was after Louis XIV, king of France, that Louisiana was named. It is fitting that I should have a dish in my repertoire named after the king who was responsible for us being here in the first place.

SEASONING

½ tsp. black pepper
½ tsp. white pepper

1 tsp. paprika
½ tsp. salt

To prepare the seasoning, combine black pepper, white pepper, paprika, and salt in a small bowl and mix together evenly.

1 tsp. solid butter or nonstick
   vegetable spray
6 8-oz. red snapper filets
Juice of 1 lemon
¾ cup white wine
2 large yellow onions

4 tbsp. clarified butter
12 jumbo mushrooms
4 tbsp. clarified butter
2 tbsp. finely chopped parsley
Lemon slices for garnish

Preheat oven to 350 degrees.

Lightly coat a baking sheet with butter or nonstick vegetable spray. Place the filets on the baking sheet and lightly sprinkle the fish with the seasoning mixture. Moisten each fish with a squeeze of lemon juice and a dash of white wine.

Slide baking sheet into heated oven and bake for 10-14 minutes, during which time, halve and slice onions into thin stips or julienne.

Heat 4 tbsp. of clarified butter in a 12-inch pan and sauté the onions for about 5 minutes or until tender and limp. At this time, rinse the mushrooms in cold water, then slice and sauté in the other 4 tbsp. clarified butter until tender (a couple of minutes).

When fish are baked, remove from oven. Place one fish filet in the center of each serving plate. Drain the excess butter from the onion sauté. Form a ring around each filet with onions, and top with equal portions of sautéed mushrooms. Sprinkle on a bit of parsley and garnish with a lemon slice. *Serves 6.*

SAUTEED TROUT LEONIE

Both my grandfather and father were named Leon, and by coincidence, my mother is named Leonie, the feminine of the name. My mother is particularly fond of artichoke bottoms and mushrooms, so I created this dish for her.

4 6-8 oz. trout filets
½ cup butter
1 cup flour
4 jumbo mushrooms, sliced

4 artichoke bottoms, cooked
   and sliced
1 tbsp. tarragon vinegar
1 lemon, cut into wedges

Melt butter in a large saucepan over a medium-low heat setting. Dredge the trout filets in flour. Pat off excess flour and sauté for 3 minutes on each side until brown. Remove and place on serving plates, keeping warm.

Add mushrooms and artichoke bottoms to the saucepan. Add the tarragon vinegar and sauté for a couple of minutes, until mushrooms are tender.

Top trout with equal portions of vegetable mixture and garnish with lemon wedges. *Serves 4.*

TROUT MARGUERY

Nicolas Marguery was a chef of note who came to the forefront of Parisian fashion during his tenure at the famous Freres Provencaux restaurant. He later opened his own restaurant in 1887, called Marguery, and served up a sole dish of the same name.

This rendition is a Creole version of the original French one, substituting trout for sole and mushrooms for mussels, which are virtually nonexistent in our waters.

2 cups Béchamel Sauce
1 cup Hollandaise Sauce
4 6-oz. trout filets
Enough water to cover

16 jumbo shrimp, boiled and
   peeled
6 large mushrooms, blanched
2 gm. truffles (optional)

Prepare Béchamel and Hollandaise sauces. Hold aside.

Roll trout filets and secure with toothpicks. Place trout rolls into a medium saucepan and fill with enough water to cover. Poach over a medium heat setting for 3 minutes. Turn off heat and keep covered.

Chop shrimp into fairly large chunks, also slice mushrooms. In a large saucepan pour in Béchamel Sauce. Fold in shrimp and mushrooms and simmer over a low heat setting for 5 minutes. Add truffles if desired.

Transfer trout rolls onto a dry cloth then place one on each plate. Remove toothpicks. Remove Béchamel Sauce from heat and gradually fold in Hollandaise Sauce until well blended. Spoon equal portions over each trout roll. *Serves 4.*

TROUT MEUNIERE AMANDINE

Gulf trout has long been one of the favored fishes of our area of the country because of its high yield of flesh to entire body weight. In this preparation, I use two traditional concepts—Meunière and Amandine—to produce a recipe that rises above the others in its complexity and in its layers of flavors and textures.

1 cup Meunière Sauce
2 cups milk
½ tsp. salt
¼ tsp. white pepper
⅛ tsp. cayenne pepper
1 egg
1 tsp. Worcestershire sauce

1 cup oil
6 8-oz. trout filets
2 cups flour
3 tbsp. sliced, toasted almonds
2 tbsp. finely chopped parsley
3 lemons, cut into wedges

Prepare the Meunière Sauce and set aside.

In a medium mixing bowl, combine the milk, salt, pepper, cayenne, egg, and Worcestershire. Mix well, using a wire whisk.

Heat oil in a heavy skillet to about 375 degrees. Lightly dust the trout filets with flour then place into the batter. Dredge the fish in the flour again. Shake off excess flour then place filets into skillet. Fry for about 3 minutes on each side, turning once. When golden brown, remove and place momentarily on a paper towel to drain.

Place one trout filet on each serving plate. Spoon on Meunière Sauce and a sprinkle of sliced toasted almonds. Garnish with finely chopped parsley and lemon wedges. *Serves 6.*

TROUT SAUTE MEUNIERE

This dish is recognized by many as one of the finest that we serve in our restaurant. The sauce complements the fresh white flesh of the trout filet, while adding a richness that is delectable.

Other fish, whole or fileted, and soft-shell crabs are also good done using this preparation.

MEUNIERE SAUCE

½ cup butter
1 tbsp. lemon juice

1 tbsp. Worcestershire sauce
2 tbsp. red wine vinegar

Melt the butter over low heat until it achieves a dark amber color. Stir in the lemon juice and Worcestershire sauce, continually stirring with a wire whisk. Add the red wine vinegar. This will cause the butter to bubble quite quickly, but continue whisking until the mixture is dark brown in color. Remove from heat.

6 trout filets
Salt to taste
Pepper to taste
½ cup clarified butter
1 cup flour

2 lemons, cut into 6 wedges, for garnish
1 tbsp. finely chopped parsley for garnish

Season trout filets with salt and pepper. To sauté trout, you may want to use 2 skillets or repeat the sauté process.

Heat clarified butter in a large skillet. Dust the trout filets in flour then sauté in the skillet over a medium heat setting for 3 minutes on each side or until golden brown. Remove onto paper towels to drain.

Place a filet on each plate, top with Meunière Sauce, and garnish with a lemon wedge and parsley. *Serves 6.*

CRABMEAT AU GRATIN

Gratin is a recipe prepared with a top crust formed by bread crumbs, grated cheese, or a mixture that is placed under a broiler or in a hot oven to crisp and seal the juices and flavors in the dish as it completes its cooking. The gratin top also adds its own texture and flavor to the dish.

Vegetables, fruits, and seafoods, especially shellfish, lend themselves deliciously to gratin dishes. This crabmeat selection is a favorite of many New Orleanians including yours truly.

3 cups Béchamel Sauce	Salt to taste
4 green onions, finely chopped	1 lb. jumbo lump crabmeat
3 tbsp. clarified butter	3 tbsp. fine bread crumbs
½ cup half & half cream	1 tsp. grated Parmesan cheese
3 egg yolks	1 tsp. chopped parsley
1 cup grated cheddar cheese	1 lemon, cut into wedges, for
Pinch cayenne pepper	garnish
¼ tsp. white pepper	

Preheat oven to 350 degrees.

Prepare Béchamel Sauce.

In a large saucepan, sauté green onions in butter over low heat setting until tender. Add the Béchamel, half & half, and egg yolks. Mix well. Add the grated cheddar cheese, and season with cayenne and white peppers, and salt to taste.

Using a wooden spoon, fold in the crabmeat and slowly simmer until hot. Arrange four oven-proof casserole dishes and spoon equal amounts of the mixture into each.

In a small bowl combine bread crumbs with Parmesan cheese and mix well. Sprinkle a coating of this mixture over each crab casserole.

Place the casseroles on a large baking sheet and bake for 15-20 minutes. Remove and garnish each with a sprinkle of parsley and a lemon wedge. *Serves 4.*

CRABMEAT RAVIGOTE

The name of this dish come from the French word to invigorate—*ravigoter*—as in the appetite. Served as appetizer or entrée, and prepared with crabmeat, as well as renditions employing shrimp, crayfish, or other garnishments, this luscious preparation piques the appetite and satisfies the palate.

This name also applies to a cold dish made with a mayonnaise base.

2 cups Béchamel Sauce	Pinch cayenne pepper
1 cup Hollandaise Sauce	¼ tsp. white pepper
4 green onions, finely chopped	Salt to taste
3 tbsp. clarified butter	1 tsp. finely chopped parsley
1 lb. jumbo lump crabmeat	

Prepare the Béchamel and Hollandaise sauces.

Sauté the green onions in clarified butter over a low heat setting until they are tender. Add the Béchamel Sauce then fold crabmeat into the sauce. Add cayenne pepper and white pepper, and salt to taste. Slowly simmer the mixture for 5 minutes. Add parsley then remove from heat.

Fold in the Hollandaise until well blended and serve in small casserole dishes. *Serves 4.*

Note: This dish can be difficult to reheat as the Hollandaise may cause it to separate. It may be best to add Hollandaise just prior to serving.

CRABMEAT ST. PIERRE

The French Catholics were particularly partial to Saint Pierre, or as we know him, Saint Peter. With all their acknowledged religious flaws, they persisted in paying homage to the saint who they believed held the keys to the gates of heaven.

Perhaps if they served up such delicious dishes as this in the name of the saint, they would be allowed to pass easily into eternal life, avoiding the pangs of purgatory and the fires of hell.

1 lb. jumbo lump crabmeat
2 large tomatoes, peeled and
  cubed
2 cups mushrooms, sliced and
  blanched
½ cup finely chopped green
  onions

2 cups Fish Stock
4 cloves garlic, minced
Salt to taste
½ tsp. white pepper
2 tbsp. finely chopped parsley

In a medium-sized earthenware pot, combine the crabmeat, tomatoes, mushrooms, green onions, and Fish Stock. Bring to a simmer over a medium-low heat setting. Add garlic and season with salt, pepper, and parsley. Over a medium-low heat setting, allow to simmer for 20 minutes. Serve hot in individual casserole dishes. *Serves 4.*

CRABMEAT SARDOU

The French playwright Victorien Sardou visited New Orleans on a voyage across the United States in the 1880s. The theater life of New Orleans was one of America's finest and most well established, and a place that Sardou was happy to have his work performed on stage.

From the performance of New Orleans first theatrical production, "La Pere Indian," in the governor's home, New Orleans had a long-standing love for the theater.

During Sardou's visit, he was fêted by the actors and theater owners of the city and this delightful supper entry was devised in his honor.

Originally the dish was served as a late after-theater supper and employed poached eggs where this recipe calls for crabmeat. My crabmeat version is one that is enjoyed equally, if not more so, than the original.

1 cup Hollandaise Sauce
1 cup Creamed Spinach
8 artichokes
Enough water to cover

1 lb. jumbo lump crabmet
2 tbsp. clarified butter
2 pinches paprika

Prepare the Hollandaise Sauce, put aside.

Prepare the Creamed Spinach. Keep warm.

Place the artichokes into a medium-sized pot filled with enough water to cover. Put a lid on the pot and boil for 30 minutes over a medium heat setting. Remove from the water and allow to cool. Peel the leaves from the artichokes, reserve for other use, or discard. Remove the hearts and using a spoon, remove and discard the choke. Slice off the remaining portions of the stems from the bottoms.

Sauté the crabmeat in the clarified butter over a medium heat setting until hot. Remove from heat and drain off excess butter.

Arrange four serving plates, spoon equal portions of Creamed Spinach onto each, then lay 2 artichoke bottoms over each spinach bed. Spoon equal portions of crabmeat over the bottoms then top with a serving spoon of Hollandaise Sauce. Garnish with a light sprinkle of paprika. *Serves 4.*

CRABMEAT YVONNE

This dish was named after my cousin Yvonne Galatoire Wynne, who has spent more than fifty years as a principal member of the Galatoire Restaurant management group.

1 lb. fresh mushrooms, washed and sliced
½ cup plus 2 tbsp. clarified butter
2 lb. backfin lump crabmeat
Salt to taste
Pepper to taste
6 fresh, boiled, sliced artichoke bottoms
6 toast points
2 tbsp. finely chopped parsley
6 lemon wedges

In a large skillet, sauté the mushrooms in the clarified butter for 10-15 minutes or until liquid rendered is reduced to a thick sauce. Add the crabmeat, and season with salt and pepper. Then add the sliced artichoke bottoms, and sauté gently until thoroughly heated.

Serve over toast points, garnishing the plates with parsley and lemon wedges. *Serves 6.*

CRABMEAT AND OYSTER PASTA

After so many years of being treated as a second-rate product, pasta emerged in New Orleans—as in the rest of the country—as the "new" hot menu item. But if you look around the old walls in the Vieux Carré, the French Quarter, you can still find the faded names of several pasta factories that were once so prominent here.

Inevitably, I choose a seafood pasta as my entry.

Olive oil, to cover pan or
   cooking surface
3 green onions, finely chopped
1 dozen sun-dried tomatoes,
   julienned
2 dozen oysters
1 bay leaf
2 tbsp. Pernod
4 sprigs parsley, finely
   chopped

2 cloves garlic, minced
¼ cup butter
Salt to taste
Pepper to taste
1 lb. jumbo lump crabmeat
1 pt. heavy cream (reserve ¼
   cup)
1 lb. linguini, or other pasta
½ cup grated Parmesan cheese

In a large skillet or saucepan, heat the olive oil on medium heat and add the green onions and tomatoes. Sauté until tender. Add the oysters, bay leaf, and Pernod. Simmer for about 3 minutes and sprinkle in the parsley and garlic. Slowly stir in the butter, seasoning to taste with salt and pepper.

Carefully add the crabmeat. Now fold the heavy cream into the crab and oyster mixture so as not to break up the crabmeat. Allow this to simmer for 10-15 minutes at a low heat until the sauce achieves a nice, thick consistency.

Cook the pasta in salted boiling water during this time for 12-15 minutes, and drain.

Serve the oyster and crabmeat mixture over the pasta. Sprinkle on the Parmesan cheese. *Serves 6-8.*

Note: You may want to use the reserved ¼ cup of cream to incorporate into the sauce to "loosen" it up if it's a bit too thick.

CRAB AND SHRIMP ZEPHYR

Years ago, when I was a child and through my teenage life, New Orleans was home to a wonderful amusement park on the shores of Lake Pontchartrain called Pontchartrain Beach. In addition to being the only well-maintained sand beach in the city, Pontchartrain Beach offered skill games, entertainments, concessions, and thrill rides that lasted the warmer months of the years, which provided us with a summer carnival of continuous attractions.

The greatest attraction of them all, and the one that separated the children from the grown-ups, was a terrifying roller coaster called the Zephyr, named after the wind of the same appellation. Proclaimed as one of the most frightening roller coasters in the South, the Zephyr was the scourge of every young boy who wanted to impress his girlfriend with his bravery.

1 green bell pepper	1 lb. shrimp
1 red bell pepper	¼ tsp. cracked black pepper
2 medium yellow onions, sliced	1 lb. jumbo lump crabmeat
	1 cup sliced mushrooms
¼ cup olive oil	3 cloves garlic, minced

Remove the seeds and pulp from the bell peppers then slice into thin julienne strips. Slice onions.

In a large sauté pan heat the olive oil over a medium-low heat setting. Add the peppers and onions and sauté for 3 minutes. Add the shrimp and season with cracked pepper and sauté until pink. Add the crabmeat and mushrooms and sauté until the mushrooms are tender. Add the minced garlic, toss, and serve. *Serves 6-8.*

FRIED SOFT-SHELL CRABS

One of the more common methods of cooking in New Orleans is frying. And one of the more delicious of our bounty of seafood items is the soft-shell crab. There is no denying that the crispness of texture and nutty fry flavor imparted by the frying greatly enhances the flavor of this seafood.

1 qt. cooking oil	2 cups flour
4 jumbo soft-shell crabs	

BATTER

1 egg	Pepper to taste
2 cups milk	

Mix ingredients together to form batter.

Salt to taste	2 lemon wedges
1 tsp. parsley	

Preheat oil in a heavy pot or deep fryer to 375 degrees over a medium heat setting.

Clean the crabs by removing the underbelly flaps, eyes, and gills located under each side of the upper shell. Dredge in flour, then shake off excess and pass thoroughly through the batter, then back into the flour and again shake off excess. Hold the crab by each claw and carefully place into the hot oil, a pair at a time. It may be necessary to do one batch at a time to accommodate the pot properly and allow the crabs space to prevent them from sticking together.

Using tongs, turn the crabs on both sides to cook evenly until golden brown (about 7-8 minutes). Remove and hold on a dry cloth, then repeat the process.

Place a pair on each plate, salt to taste, and garnish with a sprinkle of parsley and lemon wedges. *Serves 2 as an entrée, 4 as an appetizer.*

SOFT-SHELL CRABS SAUTE MEUNIERE

The simple preparation of a dish *à la meunière* comes from a light dusting of flour, where *meunière* means "the wheat miller's wife."

In New Orleans, the preparation has taken on a more substantial coating before the cooking of the fish, soft-shelled crab, or whatever products you decide to use. Fish and seafood are usually employed in this preparation, while white baby veal and escallops of chicken breast make good renditions, along with another popular dish, Frogs' Legs Meunière.

½ cup clarified butter	1 lemon (cut into 4 wedges)
½ cup Meunière Sauce	Salt to taste
1 tbsp. finely chopped parsley	Pepper to taste

Clean the crabs by removing the gills on the sides of each crab. Also, remove the flap located on the underbellies. Lightly flour each crab on a baking sheet.

Heat equal amounts of butter in two large sauté pans. Place the crabs belly up in the pans (4 to each pan). Sauté for 3 minutes on each side until nicely browned.

Remove from pans and place belly up, facing opposite directions on each serving plate. Top with 1 tbsp. Meunière Sauce on each crab. Garnish with lemon wedge and a pinch of finely chopped parsley on each crab. Season with salt and pepper to taste. *Serves 4.*

SOFT-SHELL CRAB ZACHARY

Another of my entries in this collection is named after my good friend, Zachary Richard—Cajun entertainer, songwriter extraordinaire, and culinary afficionado.

The combination of the bread crumb and Parmesan coating sautéed in butter is nicely broken by the freshness of the orange slice placed into the crab before serving.

⅔ cup fine bread crumbs
1⅓ cup yellow corn flour
½ cup finely grated Parmesan
    cheese
2 whole eggs
2 cups cold milk
8 medium-sized soft-shell
    crabs

2 cups all-purpose flour
½ cup clarified butter
1 orange, cut into 8 thin slices
2 tbsp. finely chopped parsley
Salt to taste
Pepper to taste

In a mixing bowl, combine the fine bread crumbs, yellow corn flour, and Parmesan cheese and blend well. In a separate bowl, prepare a simple milk/egg wash by beating the eggs together with the cold milk.

Clean the crabs by removing the gills from each side of each crab, remove the eyes and the flaps from the underbellies. Using a baking sheet, lightly flour each crab. Then pass the crabs through the milk/egg wash and bread evenly with the yellow corn flour/bread crumb mixture.

In two large skillets, heat equal amounts of clarified butter (¼ cup in each). When hot, place 4 crabs, belly side up, in each pan. Sauté approximately 3 minutes on each side until nicely browned.

Remove from fire and place 2 crabs on each serving plate, belly side up, and facing opposite directions. Make a cross sectional cut on each and wedge a halved slice of orange in each cut. Sprinkle a pinch of chopped parsley on each crab. Season with salt and pepper to taste. *Serves 4.*

CRAWFISH CARDINAL

The name *cardinal* comes from the red color of the sauce that early in culinary history was thought to resemble the red color of the cardinal's robes. Many dishes are called cardinal from appetizers to desserts, seafood to sweets, all being various shades of red.

In Creole culinary parlance, the best-known dish is Crawfish Cardinal.

6 cups water	1 oz. peanut oil
2 bay leaves	1 cup chopped yellow onion
1 tsp. lobster base	4 tsp. flour
1 lb. fresh crawfish tails	1 cup half & half cream
Pinch black pepper	Salt to taste
Pinch white pepper	1 cup chopped green onions
Pinch cayenne pepper	1 tsp. minced parlic
1 tbsp. paprika	3 tbsp. finely chopped parsley

Prepare a stock by bringing the water to a boil. Add bay leaves and lobster base. Allow to boil for about 20 minutes or the time it takes to yield 5 cups of stock.

In a mixing bowl, combine the crawfish tails with the peppers. Add the paprika and mix together well.

In a medium-sized pot, heat the peanut oil at a near high heat setting. The oil will be hot, but avoid any scorching. Add the chopped yellow onion and stir until tender. Add the crawfish tails and turn until the tails get hot and attain a good bond with their fat. Add flour and mix well.

Pour in the cream gradually, stirring constantly, until the sauce achieves a nice thickness and consistency. Salt to taste. Add the green onions, garlic, and parsley. Reduce the heat to a medium heat setting and simmer for about 10 minutes. *Serves 6.*

CRAWFISH ÉTOUFFÉE

From early on, the French, the Louisiana Indians, and the Spanish—our principal contributors to the development of Creole cookery—were fond of the process called *étouffée,* meaning "to smother." Much of the food and many of the early dishes were "smothered." Today an étouffée is still a smothered dish, but most commonly refers to a crawfish or shrimp stewlike concoction.

This recipe, although it calls for crawfish, can be used to prepare shrimp, oysters, mussels, scallops. . . . Whatever you have available becomes the dish.

I am particularly fond of this recipe because it was taught to me by a waiter at Galatoire's of years past, Nelson Marcotte, who was considered the master of the dish.

6 cups water	1 oz. peanut oil
2 bay leaves	1 cup chopped yellow onion
1 tsp. lobster base	4 tsp. flour
1 lb. fresh crawfish tail meat	Salt to taste
Pinch black pepper	1 cup chopped green onions
Pinch white pepper	1 tsp. minced garlic
Pinch cayenne	3 tbsp. finely chopped parsley
1 tbsp. paprika	6 cups cooked white rice

Prepare a stock by bringing the water to a boil. Add bay leaves and lobster base. Allow to boil for about 20 minutes or until the water has reduced to 5 cups of stock. Hold aside.

In a mixing bowl, combine the crawfish tails with black, white, and cayenne pepper. Add the paprika and stir together well.

In a medium-sized pot, heat the peanut oil at a near high setting. Oil should be hot but not smoking. Add the chopped yellow onion and stir until translucent. Add the crawfish tails and stir until they are heated and cooked through and have attained a good bond with their fat. Add flour and mix well.

Pour in stock gradually, stirring constantly, until sauce achieves a substantial thickness and consistency. Season with salt to taste.

Add the green onions, garlic, and parsley. Reduce the heat to a medium setting and simmer for about 10 minutes more. Serve over a bed of cooked white rice. Serves 6.

Note: If desired, you may stir in 2-3 tbsp. of butter to completed étouffée for added richness.

CRAWFISH WITH RICE AND FINE HERBS

Don't allow the simplicity of this preparation convince you that it is anything less than absolutely delicious. From early on in the city of New Orleans, both crawfish and rice were important food-stuffs in the Creole larder. It follows that a dish as basic as this, which I have devised for myself, was also a pleasant repast for the people who built this city.

The simplicity and variability of this recipe also can easily accommodate the ideas of any cook or chef. Other herbs, as well as other ingredients, can be used to alter or change the recipe to one's own liking. Other rices can be used such as popcorn, brown, or a wild and white rice mixture. Other seafood can be used such as crabmeat, shrimp, or even a filet of fish that has been cut into bite-sized pieces.

2 lb. crawfish tails	½ cup finely chopped green
½ tsp. black pepper	onions
Pinch cayenne pepper, or to	1 tbsp. minced garlic
taste	2 cups cooked rice
½ tsp. salt	2 tbsp. finely chopped parsley
¼ cup vegetable oil	½ tsp. dried tarragon
½ cup finely chopped yellow	½ tsp. dried basil
onion	

In a mixing bowl, season the crawfish tails with black pepper, cayenne pepper, and salt.

In a large sauté pan, heat the vegetable oil. Sauté the yellow onion until tender. Add the crawfish tails and green onions. Sauté this mixture for a couple of minutes, then add the garlic, rice, parsley, tarragon, and basil. Mix well and cook until piping hot. *Serves 4 generously.*

Note: This dish is traditionally spicy. I recommend flavoring with cayenne pepper or, for an interesting flavor, a dash of Melinda's hot sauce when served.

STUFFED EGGPLANT

This family recipe is, without a doubt, one of the most cherished eggplant recipes in the city. Many thousands of diners have enjoyed stuffed eggplant at Galatoire's and nary a single person has ever complained of it (other than for perhaps its copious portion), and everyone compliments it enthusiastically.

When dishes like this, which every customer is sure his mother or grandmother usually makes better, are lauded as frequently as this rendering, I know I am are doing something very special.

1 large eggplant	Salt to taste
1 cup water	⅛ tsp. white pepper
Dash red wine vinegar	Pinch cayenne pepper
½ cup clarified butter	3 tbsp. finely chopped parsley,
(reserving half for later)	reserving 1 tbsp. for garnish
4 tbsp. chopped green onions	2 tbsp. fine bread crumbs
1 cup chopped shrimp, boiled	mixed with 1 tbsp. grated
and peeled	Parmesan cheese
1 cup jumbo lump crabmeat	4 lemon wedges
1 cup Béchamel Sauce	

Preheat oven to 350 degrees.

Cut the stem off the eggplant, then slice lengthwise into 4 sections. Place into an 8 x 10 baking dish with the water and red wine vinegar. Cover with foil and bake for about 25 minutes until tender. Remove and allow to cool. Carefully remove pulp, keeping skin intact for stuffing.

In a saucepan, sauté the green onions in half of the clarified butter (¼ cup) over a low heat setting until tender. Chop the eggplant pulp and add it to the pan. Add the chopped shrimp and crabmeat and slowly simmer. Fold in the Béchamel Sauce and season with salt, white pepper, cayenne pepper, and 2 tbsp. parsley. Allow mixture to cool completely, as this will cause it to thicken and become easier to stuff.

Spoon an equal amount of stuffing into each eggplant shell. Sprinkle with bread crumb and cheese mixture, dot with remaining clarified butter, and bake at 350 degrees for 20 minutes until golden brown.

Garnish with the reserved parsley and a wedge of lemon. *Serves 4.*

FROGS' LEGS BORDELAISE WITH CEPES

In Bordeaux, where the world's most magnificent wines are produced, there are two dishes that are commonly prepared in every household as well as every roadside inn. Those two dishes are snails' and frogs' legs Bordelaise, meaning in the fashion of the Bordeaux wife/cook.

In my recipe I add cepes to enhance the dish and to multiply the texture and tastes. It is not necessary that you use cepes. Any mushrooms, fresh or rehydrated, will work.

8 pairs medium frogs' legs	1 cup clarified butter
4 cups milk	1 cup Bordelaise Sauce
¼ tsp. salt	8 large cepes or 1 15-oz. can
¼ tsp. white pepper	cepes
2 cups flour	

In a large bowl, place the frogs' legs in milk and refrigerate for 1 hour. Drain and season with salt and pepper. Dredge frogs' legs in flour and in a large skillet, slowly sauté in clarified butter over a medium-low heat setting until golden brown. Transfer to a dry cloth then to a warming place.

Prepare a Bordelaise Sauce, add sliced cepes, then return frogs' legs to sauté again for 2 minutes. Transfer to serving plates and pour sauce over frogs' legs. *Serves 4.*

FROGS' LEGS MEUNIERE

A la meunière is a preparation that is used more traditionally with fish, yet I find that using it with frogs' legs makes a delicious departure from that more common cousin.

This preparation is simple yet delicious. It is one that you will find yourself making often for relaxed and easy dinners with friends.

8 pairs small or medium frogs'
  legs
½ cup vegetable oil
Salt to taste
½ tbsp. fresh cracked black
  pepper

½ cup butter, softened
Dash tarragon vinegar
2 tsp. lemon juice
1 cup Meuniere Sauce
1 tbsp. parsley, finely chopped

Coat frogs' legs with vegetable oil then season with salt and pepper. In a large sauté pan slowly sauté over a low heat setting in softened butter until brown. Add tarragon vinegar and lemon juice. Continue to sauté for 3 minutes.

Transfer legs to serving plates then pour equal amounts of Meunière Sauce over the frogs' legs. Garnish with a sprinkle of parsley. *Serves 4.*

Note: The smaller variety of frogs' legs are more tasty and tender.

CAJUN LOBSTER BOIL

This is a good traditional recipe for a crawfish boil, where I use lobster. After all, in some areas of the country, lobsters are easier to come by than crawfish, and even in New Orleans we enjoy an occasional break from the regular fare.

4 gallons water
½ cup salt
2 pkg. "crawfish boil"
1 pod whole garlic, peeled

4 lemons, halved
1 lb. new potatoes
4 ears white corn
4 2-lb. lobsters

BUTTER GARLIC SAUCE

1 cup clarified butter
4 cloves minced garlic

1 tsp. chopped parsley

Combine the butter, garlic, and parsley to serve over the lobsters.

In a large soup pot, bring the salted water to a rolling boil. Season with the "crawfish boil" or any commercially packaged seasoning for a 10-lb. crawfish boil. Add garlic, lemon, new potatoes, and corn.

When water returns to a boil, plunge lobsters head first into pot. Boil for 15 minutes then turn off heat and allow to soak for 10 minutes. Drain off water then divide into four portions. Serve with the hot, melted Butter Garlic Sauce. *Serves 4.*

LOBSTER MEDALLIONS WITH PINK PEPPERCORNS AND CRAWFISH SEAFOOD CREAM

Although lobsters are not one of our local seafood products, we do enjoy it whenever possible. The marriage between the Maine cousin to our crawfish creates an unusually delightful harmony of flavor.

Enough salted water to cover 2
   lobsters
2 1½-lb. Maine lobsters
2 tbsp. clarified butter
1 cup crawfish tails
2 tbsp. brandy
Salt to taste

Pinch cayenne pepper
1 tsp. pink peppercorns,
   cracked
1½ cups heavy cream
2 tbsp. softened butter
2 lemon wedges

In a large soup pot, bring salted water to a rolling boil. Plunge lobsters head first into boiling water. Cover and allow to cook for 15 minutes. Remove and set aside to cool enough to handle.

Separate lobster tails from head and body section. Using a pair of boning scissors, split the underbelly with a lengthwise incision to remove the tails intact. Slice the tail meat into about 6 even rounds each. Carefully crack the claws and remove claw meat intact. Place meat aside.

In a large sauté pan, heat the clarified butter. Add the crawfish tails and lobster medallions and sauté for 2 minutes. Pour off excess butter then deglaze the pan with brandy. Flame the combination until flame is exhausted. Season with salt, cayenne pepper, and pink peppercorns. Remove only the lobster medallions. Place aside then add cream to crawfish. Reduce heat to a simmer and reduce cream by half.

Arrange the lobster medallions on each serving plate in a fan. Remove crawfish sauce from heat, swirl in softened butter, then spoon equal portions of mixture to the side of each medallion arrangement. Garnish the sides of each plate with the lobster claw meat and a wedge of lemon. *Serves 2.*

BOOLIE'S OYSTER DRESSING

It was my grandmother, Boolie Evans, who served the best oyster dressing in my memory at family gatherings for Thanksgiving and Christmas.

The recipe was passed on through the family and I have duplicated it exactly according to her own notes.

3 yellow onions	Salt to taste
4 bunches green onions	Pepper to taste
1 green bell pepper	⅛ tsp. ground bay leaf
2 whole stalks celery	1 turkey liver and heart, boiled
1 head garlic, minced	and chopped fine
1 bunch parsley, chopped fine	2 loaves stale French bread
2 tbsp. oil	6 dozen oysters and their water,
2 tbsp. butter	each cut in half

Chop all vegetables very fine. In a large, heavy-bottom skillet, heat the oil and butter over a medium-low heat setting. Add yellow onion, green onions, bell pepper, and celery. Sauté until tender. Add garlic and parsley, then season mixture with salt, pepper, and ground bay leaf. Add chopped turkey liver and heart.

Moisten the soft part of the French bread with oyster water. Squeeze thoroughly until you have about 2 cups. Add bread to skillet, mixing well. Add oysters and their water. Season again to taste.

Allow mixture to cook slowly, stirring occasionally, until oyster liquid has reduced and evaporated. For a drier dressing, you may place it in the oven at 350 degrees for 15-20 minutes. Dressing is now ready for stuffing. *Makes enough to stuff a 15-lb. turkey.*

PANEED OYSTERS BEARNAISE
WITH SALMON ROE

Rich. This is definitely a rich and luxurious presentation of oysters. Serve it Saturday night when you have all of Sunday to work it off.

2 cups Béarnaise Sauce	2 dozen oysters
½ cup fine bread crumbs	1 cup vegetable oil
½ cup yellow corn flour	4 tsp. salmon roe

Prepare Béarnaise Sauce.

Combine the bread crumbs and yellow corn flour. Dredge the oysters into this mixture.

Pan fry the oysters in oil until golden brown. Transfer to paper towels then to serving plates and top with Béarnaise and a garnish of salmon roe. *Serves 4.*

PANEED OYSTERS MEUNIERE

The bread crumb and corn flour coating is a very old-fashioned Creole device. When you try it, you will understand why we continue to use it. Oysters prepared this way also make a super po' boy sandwich.

⅓ cup fine bread crumbs	4 tbsp. Meunière Sauce
⅔ cup yellow corn flour	½ lemon, cut into 2 wedges
4 tbsp. clarified butter	1 tsp. finely chopped parsley
24 freshly shucked oysters	

Combine the bread crumbs with the yellow corn flour in a bowl and mix well.

In a large sauté pan or skillet, heat the clarified butter. Coat the oysters evenly with the flour/bread crumb mixture and place in the heated butter. Pan fry for 1½ minutes on each side or until the oysters are golden brown. Remove from the pan onto a paper towel to absorb excess butter.

Arrange on serving plates and top with 2 tbsp. Meunière Sauce per serving. Garnish with a lemon wedge and chopped parsley. *Serves 2.*

Note: The size of the oyster will affect its cooking time. Compensate by extending time for larger oysters.

OYSTER BONNE FEMME

This is a traditional French country dish that I have fashioned into a Louisiana creation. The flavors of bacon with oysters and onion, and a hint of garlic, are fabulous.

Bonne femme translates into "good woman." No one will doubt it after trying this recipe.

2 cups cooking oil	**⅓ cup bread crumbs**
2 Idaho potatoes	**4 dozen oysters**
½ lb. bacon	**2 cloves minced garlic**
2 small yellow onions	**1 tbsp. parsley**
⅔ cup yellow corn flour	

Preheat oil in a heavy frying skillet.

Cube the potatoes into ½-inch squares, then in a sauté pan, fry in hot oil until brown. Place on paper towels. Cut the bacon into 1-inch squares and fry until crisp, then place on a paper towel to drain. In a sauté pan, sauté the onions until tender, drain the excess butter, and hold aside in a warm place.

In a mixing bowl, combine the yellow corn flour and bread crumbs and blend well. Dredge the oysters in the bread crumb mixture, coating them evenly, then place into skillet of hot oil. It may be necessary to fry the oysters in 2 or 3 batches. Fry for 2 minutes on each side until golden brown. Remove with a slotted spoon then transfer to paper towels. Reheat the onions and add garlic.

Arrange 1 dozen oysters per serving plate, then top with onions, potatoes, and bacon. Garnish with parsley. *Serves 4.*

OYSTER PAN ROAST

This is a delicious way to conserve the luscious juices of the oysters so that they will be incorporated into the other ingredients as they all simmer together and roast in the oven.

Although I serve this dish as an appetizer, it serves well as an entrée with just a small salad and a loaf of hot French bread to soak up the pan juices.

2 cups water
2 dozen oysters in their water
2 tbsp. clarified butter
⅓ cup finely chopped green
    onions
2 tbsp. flour
Pinch thyme

Pinch bay leaf powder
Salt to taste
⅛ tsp. white pepper
2 egg yolks
2 tbsp. fine bread crumbs
    mixed with 1 tsp. grated
    Parmesan cheese

Preheat oven to 350 degrees.

In a small pot, bring the water to a boil. Add the oysters in their liquid and boil until the edges curl (about 5 minutes). Remove the oysters using a slotted spoon and arrange 6 oysters in each of four individual casserole dishes. Reserve liquid for sauce.

In a large saucepan, in the clarified butter, sauté the green onions until tender over a medium heat setting. Sprinkle in flour while constantly stirring using a wooden spoon until roux is hot. Gradually pour in oyster liquid and stir until sauce thickens. Season with thyme, bay leaf powder, salt, and white pepper. Remove from heat, stir in egg yolks, then cover each portion of oysters with sauce.

Sprinkle with the bread crumb/cheese mixture and bake for 15-20 minutes. *Serves 4.*

Note: This recipe is also included as an appetizer.

FRIED OYSTERS

This is a most traditional method using the crumbs from stale French bread and corn flour as the fry coating. These ingredients work marvelously well with the oysters, giving them a nutty flavor that enhances their own quite well.

This same recipe works equally well with shrimp.

⅓ cup bread crumbs
⅔ cup yellow corn flour
2 cups vegetable oil
2 dozen oysters
Salt to taste

Pepper to taste
Choice of condiments, usually
    either cocktail sauce or tartar
    sauce
Lemon wedges

In a mixing bowl, combine the bread crumbs and yellow corn flour and blend well.

In a heavy skillet, heat the oil over a medium heat setting (about 375 degrees). Dredge the oysters into the bread crumb mixture coating evenly and place into the hot oil. Cook for approximately 2 minutes on each side or until golden brown. Remove and transfer oysters to paper towels to absorb the excess oil. It may be necessary to cook 2 separate batches.

Season the oysters with salt and pepper to taste and serve with condiments of cocktail sauce or tartar sauce. Garnish with lemon wedges. *Serves 4.*

SHRIMP CESAR

This recipe is actually a creation of one of our most popular waiters at Galatoire's—Cesar. As often happens, a regular customer wanted something "different," and Cesar concocted this dish for him.

3 dozen jumbo shrimp
1 bay leaf
1 tsp. salt
Pinch cayenne pepper
3 cups water (for shrimp stock)
½ cup butter, softened
6 artichoke bottoms, sliced

6 large mushrooms, sliced
3 tbsp. finely chopped green
    onions
¼ cup white wine
1 tsp. minced garlic
3 cups cooked rice

Peel the shrimp, reserving the heads and shells for stock. In a small pot, combine shrimp peels, bay leaf, salt, and cayenne pepper with the water and boil for 20 minutes. Strain the liquid through a fine sieve.

At a medium setting, melt 4 tbsp. of the softened butter in a large saucepan or shallow pot and sauté the sliced artichoke bottoms, mushrooms, and green onions until tender. Add the shrimp and sauté until pink and firm. Add the white wine and stir. Add the shrimp stock and allow to simmer and reduce for approximately 5 minutes.

Add the garlic and stir. Remove from heat and swirl in the remaining butter. Sauce will begin to thicken; blend well and serve over rice. *Serves 6.*

Note: See recipe for Trout Leonie as a reference for cooking and preparing artichokes.

SHRIMP CLEMENCEAU

Clemenceau became the premier of France in 1906. This dish was invented in New Orleans to honor him.

The original, however, was made with chicken, which can also be found in this collection. Here I use shrimp as the main ingredient.

2 Idaho potatoes, cut and fried as in Potatoes Brabant	6 jumbo mushrooms, or 2 cups, sliced
½ cup clarified butter	4 cloves garlic, minced
4 dozen jumbo shrimp, boiled and peeled	½ tsp. cracked black pepper
	1 15-oz. can early peas

Prepare Potatoes Brabant, omitting garlic and butter.

Heat the clarified butter in a large sauté pan over medium heat. Sauté shrimp until pink. Add mushrooms and continue to cook until tender. Add garlic, black pepper, and potatoes. Drain excess butter, add peas to heat, and then serve. *Serves 4.*

SHRIMP CREOLE

This is a most important dish, perhaps the single most important. Many restaurants are judged by their Creole dishes, and locals know a good Sauce Creole when it is served to them.

The word *Creole* is used to designate the descendants of the French and Spanish who came to Louisiana to build a new life for themselves, and in doing so, built a most unusual American culture. Imbued with the Latin fervor for love and food, the Creoles of New Orleans paid great attention to the fare presented on their tables.

This particular recipe shines brightly with the influence of the Spanish who returned to Louisiana the great use of tomatoes and sweet green peppers that were part of the treasure brought to Europe by Columbus's followers.

The recipe for the Creole Sauce should be followed closely to be sure that it comes out properly.

2 lb. jumbo shrimp, boiled and peeled

4 cups Creole Sauce
4 cups cooked rice

In a large saucepan, combine the Creole Sauce and shrimp and simmer for 5 minutes to heat. Serve over a circle of rice. *Serves 4-6.*

CARIBBEAN GRILLED SHRIMP

It's the Melinda's hot sauce, which is a Habanero pepper sauce (use any Habanero pepper sauce), the citrus juices, and the lime wedge garnish that really give this dish the Caribbean flavor. The flavors remind me of many evenings on many beaches on Caribbean islands during vacations.

4 dozen (48) large shrimp, 10-15
  count, peeled and deveined,
  with tail on.

MARINADE

1 tbsp. Creole mustard
2 tbsp. Melinda's (mild) hot
  sauce
1 tbsp. Worcestershire sauce
3 sprigs parsley, finely
  chopped

1 tsp. Pernod
2 tbsp. lemon juice
2 tbsp. orange juice, freshly
  squeezed
2 tbsp. vegetable oil

¼ cup butter

1 clove garlic, minced

Butterfly the shrimp with tail on by making a careful lengthwise cut down the back from head to tail. Rinse in cold water and put aside.

Combine the marinade ingredients in a bowl. Using a wire whisk, mix together well and fold in the shrimp, covering well. Refrigerate for one hour.

In a small saucepan, melt the butter and garlic on a low flame, then prepare to baste the shrimp.

Using a gas or charcoal grill at about medium heat, place the shrimp on the grill for about two minutes on each side, basting constantly with the garlic butter sauce.

Serve with a lime wedge, which truly enhances the flavor and character of the Caribbean. *Serves 4.*

CRACKED PEPPER SHRIMP SAUTEED WITH VEGETABLES

This dish is reminiscent of the Catalonian dishes brought here by the early Spanish settlers. Their period of dominancy of the colony of New Orleans was from 1764 to 1803. Their powerful influence remains today in the architecture as well as the cuisine.

This simple yet delectable recipe is one that I myself have concocted. It is light, delicious, and uncomplicated to prepare. It is the kind of dish I provide for myself and my friends after a long, hot day at the restaurant stove.

1 bell pepper	⅓ tsp. cracked black peppercorns
1 small yellow onion	
4 large fresh mushrooms	2 tbsp. Pernod
2 tbsp. softened butter	½ tsp. minced garlic
2 tbsp. olive oil	1 lemon, quartered, for garnish
3 dozen large peeled shrimp	

Halve the bell pepper lengthwise, remove seeds and pulp. Peel and remove ends from onion. Cut both bell pepper and onion into julienne strips. Slice mushrooms.

Melt the butter into a medium-sized saucepan. Sauté the vegetables until tender then remove from heat and set aside.

In a separate, larger pan, heat the olive oil. When hot, add the shrimp along with the cracked peppercorns. Sauté until the shrimp are pink and firm. Add the Pernod. Cook out the alcohol—a few seconds—add the shrimp and cook and combine the vegetables with the shrimp until both are hot.

Add the minced garlic, stir, and serve. Garnish with lemon wedges. *Serves 4 generously.*

SHRIMP ÉTOUFFÉE

The word étouffée simply means "to smother." In Creole cookery everything eventually gets into the étouffée pot.

48 jumbo shrimp	3 tsp. flour
5 cups water	1 4-oz. can tomato sauce
2 bay leaves	1 tsp. minced garlic
2 tbsp. peanut oil	3 tsp. finely chopped parsley
1 cup finely chopped yellow onion	Pinch black pepper
	Pinch white pepper
1 cup finely chopped green onions	Pinch cayenne
	3 cups cooked rice

Peel the shrimp, reserving the heads and shells. In a small pot, add the water for the stock, along with the bay leaves, shrimp heads, and shells. Boil stock for 15-20 minutes, ideally reducing the stock to yield no less than 4 cups of stock for the sauce. Strain the stock through a fine sieve.

In a shallow pot, heat the peanut oil on a medium setting allowing the oil to get hot but not scorched. Add the yellow onion and stir until tender, then add the shrimp, stirring them until they become pink and firm.

Fold in the green onions and sauté for 3 minutes. Sprinkle in the flour and blend well.

Pour in the 4 cups of hot stock and stir until sauce begins to thicken, then stir in the tomato sauce followed by garlic, parsley, and seasonings. Allow to simmer on a reduced heat setting long enough to achieve a nice, thick consistency.

Serve over a bed of cooked rice. *Serves 6.*

Note: Traditionally this is a rather well-seasoned dish. I recommend to season to taste, favoring black pepper.

STEWED SHRIMP COURT BOUILLON

Court bouillon means "short boil." Yet in New Orleans cuisine, this has become a sort of tomato baked recipe that is served mostly with redfish, although in this particular recipe I like to use shrimp for a different and perhaps more interesting presentation.

This dish is a staple of Creole cuisine.

48 large shrimp
3 whole peeled tomatoes
3 yellow onions
2 bell peppers
6 tbsp. olive oil

3 cloves minced garlic
4 cups Shrimp Stock (recipe below)
3 cups cooked rice

STOCK INGREDIENTS

Shrimp heads and shells
1 qt. salted water
1 carrot, julienned
2 ribs celery, chopped

1 large onion, quartered
2 bay leaves
1 tbsp. whole black peppercorns

To make the stock, peel and remove the heads from the shrimp and reserve them. Rinse the shrimp and put aside.

Fill a soup pot with the salted water and heat on a high setting. Put in the heads and shells, julienned carrots, chopped celery, onion, bay leaves, and peppercorns. Boil uncovered for 30 minutes and strain through a fine sieve. This is the shrimp stock. Yield should be 4 cups.

Cut the tomatoes and onions into wedges, separating the onion and julienne the bell peppers. In a large saucepan or stewing pot, heat enough olive oil to thoroughly cover the cooking surface of the pot. Sauté the onion and bell peppers for 2-3 minutes until tender. Add the shrimp and sauté until they are pink and firm. Add in the tomatoes and garlic. Cook for a few minutes until they are soft, then pour in 4 cups of the shrimp stock and cover. On a medium heat setting, cook for 20 minutes during which time you may cook your rice.

Serve the court bouillon over rice. *Serves 6.*

SHRIMP MARGUERY

Invented in the late 1880s at the famous Parisian Restaurant Marguery, this dish was one that was brought to New Orleans not long after that. Although this dish is more traditionally prepared with fish—usually trout—I think it is even better when made with shrimp.

2 cups Béchamel Sauce	4 dozen jumbo shrimp, boiled
1 cup Hollandaise Sauce	and peeled
½ cup water	Salt to taste
1 cup sliced mushrooms	Pinch cayenne pepper

Prepare the Béchamel Sauce and set aside.

Prepare the Hollandaise Sauce and set aside.

Blanche the mushrooms in a small saucepan filled with ½ cup water for 2 minutes. Remove with a slotted spoon.

In a large earthenware pot, heat the Béchamel Sauce to a simmer, folding in the mushrooms and shrimp. Season with salt and pepper and slowly simmer on a low heat setting for 5 minutes. Remove from the heat and fold in the Hollandaise Sauce until blended thoroughly. Serve hot in small individual casserole dishes. *Serves 4.*

Poultry

CHICKEN BORDELAISE WITH CEPES

The French settlers of Bordeaux brought the use of this garlic sauce to the Province of Louisiana. Subsequently the Spanish who came employed garlic heavily in their cuisine, while finally the Italian influx of the early twentieth century firmly rooted the heavy high use of garlic in our Creole cuisine.

2 1½-lb. spring chickens	½ cup clarified butter
½ cup vegetable oil	1 tbsp. minced garlic
½ tsp. salt	1 tbsp. chopped parsley
1 tsp. white pepper	8 large cepes (or 15-oz. can)

Preheat oven to 400 degrees.

Rinse chickens with cold water and pat dry. Quarter chickens, discard backs, and lightly coat parts with oil. Season with salt and pepper, then place on a baking sheet and cook for 25 minutes. Remove chicken from oven and transfer to a large, oven-proof casserole.

Prepare Cepes Bordelaise by heating clarified butter in a medium saucepan. Add garlic and parsley. Cut cepes into thin slices and add to sauce. Heat, then pour combination over chicken. Cover casserole with foil and return to oven for 15 minutes.

Remove chicken from oven and place equal portions on serving plates and top with remaining juices. *Serves 4-6.*

GRILLED CHICKEN BREAST BONNE FEMME

In the style of the good woman is what *bonne femme* refers to. This simple country preparation is truly delicious. Never have I served it without getting raves from my guests.

3 Idaho potatoes, peeled and
  sliced into cottage fries
1 cup vegetable oil
4 whole chicken breasts
4 tbsp. vegetable oil
½ tsp. salt
⅓ tsp. black pepper
⅓ tsp. paprika combined with a
  pinch of cayenne pepper

¼ lb. bacon
2 tbsp. clarified butter
2 medium yellow onions,
  sliced
2 cloves garlic, pressed
2 tbsp. finely chopped parsley

Prepare the cottage fries by heating the cup of vegetable oil in a deep-well skillet over a medium heat setting (about 350 degrees). Cut the potatoes in crosswise thin slices (about ⅛ inch). Fry small bunches at a time, transferring each bunch to paper towels and lying flat. Hold potato slices until preparation of dish is almost complete, then reheat in hot oil to achieve a crisp, evenly browned potato.

Remove the skin and nuggets from the whole chicken breasts. Rinse with cold water and pat dry. Coat both sides of the chicken with the 4 tbsp. of vegetable oil and season with salt, black pepper, and paprika and cayenne mixture.

Place the chicken on a grill over a medium heat setting and cook for 4 minutes on each side, marking each side with a crisscross pattern.

During this time, fry the bacon strips in a large skillet over low heat until brown and crispy on both sides. Transfer to paper towels to drain. Remove the chicken breasts from the grill and hold aside in a warm place.

In a medium sauté pan, sauté the onions in clarified butter until light brown, add garlic, and continue to sauté for 3 minutes. Remove from the heat, drain off excess butter, and hold aside.

Arrange the chicken breasts on serving plates and top with equal portions of onions and bacon strips, then cover with a layer of cottage-fried potatoes. Garnish with a sprinkle of parsley. *Serves 4.*

GRILLED CHICKEN BREAST BLUES

If you are a blue cheese afficionado, you will die for this dish. I am a blue-cheese lover and created this recipe to indulge my palate.

Needless to say, Stilton or Roquefort, or even a smooth Bresse Bleu, can be substituted to make the recipe even more elegant.

8 chicken breast filets	¼ cup clarified butter
½ cup vegetable oil	1½ cups hot milk
½ tsp. cracked black pepper-corns	1 cup blue cheese, crumbled
Salt to taste	Juice of ½ small lemon
3 tbsp. flour	1 tbsp. lemon zest
	4 sprigs parsley

Lightly coat chicken filets with oil. Season with black pepper and salt. Grill filets over medium heat, 3 minutes on each side. Remove and hold on warm plate.

Prepare a light roux, combining equal parts flour and butter over a low heat setting. Whisk mixture until well blended. Add hot milk and whisk until sauce thickens. Add ⅔ cup of the crumbled blue cheese and stir until melted. Add lemon juice and stir.

Serve sauce over chicken filets, then sprinkle each portion with equal amounts of remaining blue cheese (⅓ cup) and lemon zest. Garnish with parsley sprigs and imagination. *Serves 4.*

BAKED CHICKEN CLEMENCEAU

George Benjamin Eugene Clemenceau was a French statesman born in 1841 who became the premier of France in 1906. This dish was created in New Orleans to honor that man.

My version employs cepes, which add a most rich garnish to the recipe.

2 1½-2 lb. fryer chickens	2 Idaho potatoes
4 cloves minced garlic, mixed with 2 tbsp. vegetable oil	1 cup vegetable oil
1 tsp. paprika	8 large jumbo mushrooms
¾ tsp. white pepper	½ cup clarified butter
1 tsp. salt	1 15-oz. can petit pois, drained

Preheat the oven to 400 degrees.

Rinse the chickens inside and out with cold water, pat dry. Quarter the chickens and lightly coat with the oil-garlic mixture. Season with paprika, white pepper, and salt. Place on a baking sheet and bake for 25-30 minutes until golden brown.

During the baking time, prepare brabant potatoes as follows:

Peel the potatoes and slice into 1-inch cubes. Heat oil in a large skillet over a medium heat setting. Add the potatoes and slowly pan fry while turning until golden brown. Remove using a slotted spoon and transfer onto paper towels. Discard or store grease. Remove the chicken from oven and keep warm.

Rinse and slice the mushrooms. Heat the clarified butter in a large saucepan over medium heat and sauté the mushrooms until tender. Add potatoes and peas (only to heat).

Place equal portions of chicken onto serving plates, drain off excess butter from vegetable sauté and top chicken servings with equal portions. *Serves 4-6.*

CHICKEN CREOLE

Employing the most "Creole" of all Creole sauces, this dish comes more from our Spanish period of domination than from the French or American periods.

It was the Spanish who introduced the heavy use of tomatoes into our cuisine, tomatoes that were discovered in the Americas more than 250 years prior to the Spaniards taking possession of New Orleans from the French.

4 cups Creole Sauce	**Salt to taste**
1 2-lb. fryer chicken	**¼ tsp. white pepper**
2 tbsp. vegetable oil	**4 cups cooked rice**

Preheat oven to 350 degrees.
Prepare Creole Sauce.
Disjoint chicken and lightly coat with oil. Season with salt and pepper and bake for 25 minutes until brown. Transfer to a large saucepan, add Creole Sauce and simmer over a medium-low heat setting for 10 minutes. Serve over rice. *Serves 4.*

GRILLED BREAST OF CHICKEN WITH MUSTARD CREAM SAUCE

In the early colony from 1718 to the turn of the nineteenth century, every colonist, every Creole, had a vegetable garden and raised chickens for the family's own use. For that reason chicken dishes make up a large segment of classic Creole recipes.

This simple dish I created as an easy and appetizing adjunct to my standard repertoire of often richer dishes. Although the sauce is cream-based, it remains light to the taste and well accompanies the freshness and delicacy of the grilled chicken.

4 whole, boneless chicken
  breasts
	1 tbsp. cracked black
	  peppercorns

2 tbsp. cooking oil	Mustard Cream Sauce

Rinse the chicken breasts under cold water; pat dry. Lightly grease both sides with cooking oil. Sprinkle an even amount of cracked black peppercorns on each side of the chicken breasts.

Place the breasts on a medium heat setting on your grill or pit. Grill for only about 3 minutes on each side to ensure moisture and tenderness. Do not overcook the chicken.

Remove from the grill and place one chicken breast on each plate. Nap the grilled chicken breasts with the warm Mustard Cream Sauce. *Serves 4.*

Note: You may purchase cracked peppercorns by the bottle. Personally, I prefer to crack them fresh, for this way they emit a more pronounced fragrance and flavor.

CHICKEN FINANCIERE

This is such a rich preparation that it is named *financière*, in the style of the finance administrator. It comes from traditional French cookery and has remained on the old restaurant menus even from the earliest days.

4 cups Marchand de Vin Sauce	4 chicken livers
2 tbsp. clarified butter	8 green oilves, seeded and sliced
1 tbsp. cooking oil	

1 2½-lb. fryer chickens,
  quartered
	1 tbsp. finely chopped parsley
	  flakes

Prepare Marchand de Vin Sauce.

In a heavy skillet, heat the butter and oil over a medium heat setting. Brown chicken parts on all sides then transfer to an earthenware pot containing the Marchand de Vin Sauce.

Sauté the chicken livers in a skillet until lightly browned and also transfer to pot with chicken. Add the olive slivers, cover the pot, and slowly simmer for 30-35 minutes. During this time, if necessary, adjust consistency by adding water.

Arrange equal portions of chicken on each serving plate, cover with sauce, and garnish with a sprinkle of parsley. *Serves 4.*

GRILLED CARIBBEAN CHICKEN IN JERK MARINADE

There is hardly a dish that is more well known from the Caribbean than "jerked" dishes. It is to the Caribbean inhabitants what our barbeque sauce is to Americans.

And don't forget the lime garnish. It is essential to the total flavor of the preparation.

½ cup finely chopped green onions
1 tbsp. red wine vinegar
1 tsp. Habanero pepper sauce
1 tbsp. soy sauce
1 jalapeño chili pepper, finely chopped
½ tbsp. ground allspice
Pinch ground nutmeg
½ tsp. ground cinnamon
Salt to taste
¼ tsp. black pepper
8 boneless chicken breast halves
1 lime, sliced

To make the marinade, combine all the ingredients except the chicken and lime in a medium mixing bowl. Mix well using a wire whisk. Add the chicken breasts coating both sides. Cover and refrigerate overnight.

Preheat a grill and cook chicken breasts over medium hot embers for 4-5 minutes on each side, basting with the marinade. Transfer to serving plates, using 2 breast halves for each plate. Garnish with lime slices. *Serves 4.*

ROAST CHICKEN MOUTARDE

In New Orleans we use Creole mustard in about as many ways as any good product can be used. In this case, I have married Creole to her French cousin Dijon to get just the right flavor.

1 2-lb. chicken	¼ cup cooking oil
2 tbsp. Dijon mustard	Salt to taste
1 tsp. Creole mustard	½ tsp. white pepper
2 cloves minced garlic	1 tsp. finely chopped parsley

Preheat oven to 350 degrees.

Rinse chicken inside and out then pat dry. Combine mustards and garlic in a small mixing bowl. Slowly dribble in oil, mixing with a wire whisk, until well blended. Season chicken inside and out with salt and pepper. Truss the chicken, then cover evenly with the mustard mixture.

Place the chicken in a roasting pan then into the oven for 35-40 minutes. Remove trussing and carve to serve. Garnish with finely chopped parsley. *Serves 2-4.*

CHICKEN ROCHAMBEAU

This marvelous and elegant rendition of Antoine Alciatore's Haute Creole classic is named after Jean Baptiste Donatien de Vimeur, Compte de Rochambeau. Rochambeau played an important role as commanding general of the French forces aiding in the American revolutionary war against the British.

The utilization of two important sauces—Béarnaise and Marchand de Vin—makes for a sublime marriage of tastes and colors.

1 cup Marchand de Vin Sauce
1 cup Béarnaise Sauce
2 whole chicken breasts,
  boneless
Salt to taste

Pepper to taste
2 cups chicken stock
¼ lb. ham, boiled (4 slices)
8 toast points

Prepare the sauces and set aside.

Split each chicken breast into halves. Butterfly each half and season with salt and pepper. Poach chicken breast in stock for 10 minutes, then add ham slices and cover to heat for 5 minutes. Remove chicken and ham, place on a dry cloth to drain.

Place a slice of ham on each serving plate. Spoon a small amount of Marchand de Vin over each slice. Arrange the chicken breasts on sauce and cover with Béarnaise. Garnish with toast points. *Serves 4.*

CHICKEN ST. PIERRE

The vegetable garnish used to produce the sauce in this dish was originally devised for use in New Orleans with the drum fish that is so available in this area: the redfish, the most celebrated of the drum family.

Although this preparation delivers an excellent fish offering, I also enjoy it as used in this chicken recipe.

CHICKEN STOCK

1 2-lb. whole fryer chicken
4 cups water
Pinch of salt

1 yellow onion, chopped
1 bay leaf

Disjoint the chicken in order to use the back and neck for the stock, reserving the remainder of the chicken for the dish. Then prepare the chicken stock by combining the above ingredients. Allow stock to boil over a medium heat setting for 25 minutes. Strain stock through a fine sieve.

Remainder of the chicken
Salt to taste
¼ tsp. black pepper
2 tbsp. shortening
2 tomatoes, peeled and cubed
½ cup green onions, finely
   chopped
1 cup sliced mushrooms
3 cloves garlic, minced
2 cups chicken stock
1 tbsp. parsley, finely chopped
2 cups cooked rice

Season the chicken pieces with salt and pepper. In a medium stewing pot, heat the shortening over a moderate flame. Add the chicken and brown on both sides. Add the tomatoes, green onions, mushrooms, and garlic. Simmer for 10 minutes.

Add 2 cups of the chicken stock and the parsley. Cover and stew for 25 minutes. Serve over steamed rice. *Serves 4.*

CHICKEN YASSA

The original recipe for this dish come from Senegalese cuisine and was used with monkey.

I prefer chicken.

Juice of 3 limes
2 yellow onions, sliced
4 cloves garlic, minced
½ tsp. salt
½ tsp. black pepper
2 chili peppers, finely chopped
¼ cup peanut oil
2 2½-lb. chickens
1 green, red, and yellow bell
   pepper, small
2 tbsp. olive oil
2 tbsp. marinade liquid
2 tbsp. soy sauce
½ cup water
6 cups cooked rice
2 tbsp. finely chopped parsley

In a mixing bowl, prepare a marinade by combining the lime juice, yellow onions, garlic, salt, black pepper, chili peppers, and peanut oil. Cut the chicken into quarters and marinate for 6 hours refrigerated. Grill over hot embers until brown on both sides. Remove and put aside.

Remove the pulp and seeds from the 3 different bell peppers. Cut each in half and grill until the skins are scorched. Remove from the spit and cut each into julienne strips. Remove the onion from the marinade and sauté in olive oil along with the bell peppers in two large skillets over a medium-low heat until the onions are translucent. Moisten the sauce with 2 tbsp. of the marinade liquid, 2 tbsp. soy sauce, and ½ cup water.

Add the chicken pieces, cover, and allow to simmer over a low heat setting for 25 minutes.

Arrange the chicken pieces on a large hot platter in a ring of rice. Baste with the sauce and garnish with bell peppers and parsley. *Serves 6.*

CHICKEN LIVERS EN BROCHETTE

There's rare a better marriage of flavors than chicken livers and bacon.

Cooked and served *en brochette*, which means "on a skewer," it becomes an easily handleable unit during the process, and can then be unskewered onto the plate at the table for a small touch of culinary theatrics.

18 strips of bacon	Dash Tabasco sauce
36 large chicken livers	2 cups cooking oil
2 cups milk	2 cups flour
1 egg	3 slices toast, cut in wedges
Pinch of salt	6 lemon wedges
⅛ tsp. white pepper	1 tbsp. finely chopped parsley

Cut each bacon strip in half. Blanch bacon in boiling water for 3 minutes. Remove and place on paper towel and pat dry.

Arrange chicken livers and bacon strips on brochette skewers, alternating one chicken liver then one bacon strip, etc., with a half-dozen on each skewer.

In a medium mixing bowl, combine the milk, egg, salt, pepper, and Tabasco to make a batter and whisk well. Preheat oil in a deep frying pan over a medium heat setting. Pour flour into a baking pan with 2-inch sides. Dip the brochettes into the batter to fully cover then dredge into flour. Shake of excess flour and place a few at a time into the frying pan. Allow brochettes to fry, turning every 2 minutes or so until firm and golden brown.

Transfer to paper towels then to serving plates. Garnish with a toast wedge, a lemon wedge, and parsley. *Serves 6.*

Note: Meunière Sauce is a beautiful complement to this dish.

CHICKEN LIVER SAUTE
WITH DIRTY RICE

Not a single product, or by-product, ever went unused in the Creole kitchen. In many cases, the secondary fruit of the principal—livers of the chicken—became even more sumptuous than the chicken itself. In this extremely simple dish, the livers are as delicious as they can be: no overdoing, no unnecessary masking of flavors. Absolutely delectable.

9 whole chicken livers	Pinch salt
4 tbsp. clarified butter	2 pinches white pepper
2 tbsp. chopped green onions	Pinch cayenne pepper
1 cup cooked rice	1 tsp. chopped parsley

Rinse the chicken livers in cold water. Drain on a dry cloth. Heat 2 tbsp. of the clarified butter in a 10-inch sauté pan or skillet. Sauté the chicken livers for 5-6 minutes on a medium-high heat setting until brown and firm but not overcooked. Hold aside warm and remove 3 of the cooked livers.

In another sauté pan heat the remaining butter. Chop the 3 livers and add them to the sauté pan with the green onions; sauté for 2 minutes.

Stir in the rice and season with salt, white pepper, and cayenne pepper. Serve the warm whole livers with equal portions of dirty rice. Garnish with a sprinkle of chopped fresh parsley. *Serves 2.*

COQ AU VIN

This is a classic French country dish that was an early entry into the kitchens of New Orleans homes.

Of all the supplies that the French were sure to have shipped with as regular a frequency as possible, it was wine and Cognac. It also was the case that every homesite in the early city of New Orleans was laid out with an ample area for gardening of essential vegetables and the raising of poultry. Coq au Vin was as natural to the cooks here as was corn to the Indians.

1 2½-lb. fryer chicken	3 cups red wine
1 bay leaf	1 cup white stock
1 yellow onion, cubed	3 cloves garlic, minced
3 cups water	⅛ tsp. thyme
¼ lb. bacon, cubed	1 bay leaf
2 tbsp. clarified butter	1 large yellow onion, chopped
½ tsp. salt	2 tbsp. clarified butter
⅛ tsp. white pepper	2 cups mushrooms, sliced
¼ cup brandy	1 tbsp. parsley, finely chopped

Disjoint chicken and reserve neck and back for white stock. Prepare stock by boiling neck and back along with the innards, bay leaf, and cubed onion in the water for 1 hour, partially covered.

In a earthenware pot, sauté the bacon cubes in clarified butter until brown. Remove to a paper towel.

Brown the chicken in the remaining hot fat in the earthenware pot. Season the chicken with the salt and white pepper. Return the bacon to the casserole with chicken. Cover and cook slowly for 10 minutes. Add the brandy and ignite it, shaking the pan back and forth until the flame is extinguished.

Pour in the red wine, 1 cup of the white stock (enough to cover the chicken). Stir in minced garlic, thyme, and bay leaf. Cover and simmer over a low heat setting for 30 minutes.

Brown the chopped onions in a sauté pan in clarified butter over medium heat. Add the mushrooms and sauté for 5 more minutes. Drain off excess butter.

Arrange the chicken parts on a hot platter. Baste with the sauce and arrange the onions and mushrooms around the chicken. Garnish with parsley. *Serves 4.*

ROAST DUCK

A good winter evening's meal is roast duck, particularly in duck hunting season, when the wild ducks are freshly come by. But, as with all good products, fine ducks are available commercially. Certainly they can become the delectable dish just as well as their wild cousins.

2 2-lb. domestic ducks	1 turnip, chopped
Salt to taste	1 head garlic, minced
Pepper to taste	1 cup water
2 tbsp. softened butter	2 cups red wine
1 tsp. thyme, dried	2 oz. duck liver pâté
2 yellow onions, sliced	

Preheat oven to 450 degrees.

Rinse ducks inside and out with cold water, then pat dry. Season with salt and pepper. Rub inside and out with the softened butter, sprinkle with thyme, and place on roasting racks on roasting pans. Place onions, turnip, and garlic at the bottom of the roasting pans. Pour in water and red wine. Place the ducks into the oven and allow them to cook at high heat for 20 minutes. Baste ducks with pan juices, then reduce heat to 350 degrees and cook for 15 minutes. Test for doneness by piercing the fleshy part of the leg to check for running blood.

Remove the ducks from the oven, reserving pan drippings for sauce. Skim surface of excess fat, then pour juices through a fine sieve to strain. In a medium saucepan, heat pan juices to a simmer over a medium heat setting. Add pâté and reduce liquid by half.

Carve the ducks, arranging the breast meat in a fan, then top with sauce. *Serves 4.*

DUCK BREAST SAUTEED IN MANGO CABERNET SAUCE

Admittedly, this is a departure from most of the fare collected here as principally Creole. It is an excellent dish of my own devise, however, and should especially please the "toney" culinarians of your group.

2 3½-4 lb. ducks
Salt to taste
¼ tsp. black pepper
⅓ cup cooking oil
1 carrot, sliced
1 small onion, chopped
2 cups white wine
Enough water to cover

2 tbsp. clarified butter
1 small ripe mango
2 tbsp. softened butter
4-5 whole shallot bulbs
1 tsp. green peppercorns
1½ cups Cabernet Sauvingnon
⅛ tsp. ground nutmeg

Bone ducks, reserving the carcass and unused parts for stock. Trim and season the breasts with salt and pepper and put aside.

In a heavy saucepan, heat the oil and add the duck bones, carrot, and onion. Cook over a medium-high heat setting until well browned. Drain off fat and deglaze the pan with white wine. Add enough water to cover the bones and vegetables by 1 inch. Reduce heat and simmer for 1½ hours very slowly.

Preheat the oven to 400 degrees.

In a sauté pan, heat the butter and place duck breasts skin down and sauté until lightly browned. This also reduces fat. Transfer the breasts from the sauté pan to a baking pan and place in the oven to cook for 10 minutes. Remove and keep warm. During the baking time, prepare the sauce.

Peel and slice the mango into strips. In a sauté pan, melt the softened butter. Add shallots and peppercorns, sautéeing until tender. Add the mango slices and cabernet. Reduce slightly then add the duck stock and nutmeg and simmer slowly for 20-30 minutes uncovered until the sauce is reduced by half.

To serve, on a small chopping board trim the bone from the duck breast and place skin-side down on the board. Slice thin diagonal slices. Pour enough sauce onto plates to cover the bottom of surface. Arrange duck slices in a fan fashion over the sauce. Arrange the mango slices at the bottom of the fanned breasts. Garnish with your choice of vegetable. *Serves 4.*

ROAST SQUAB AU FOIE GRAS

Well, this is a return to classic French cuisine. And although I have not taxed your pockets with real foie gras, the resulting dish will taste as though I have.

2 large squabs	4 bell peppers, chopped fine
Salt to taste	1 pimento, chopped fine
Pepper to taste	1 cup wild rice, cooked
1 tsp. clarified butter	1 clove minced garlic
½ cup chicken livers	½ oz. pâté de foie gras
½ cup green onions, chopped fine	1 tsp. finely chopped parsley

Preheat oven to 350 degrees.

Season the squabs inside and out with salt and pepper. Rub with softened butter. Place in a roasting dish and bake for 25 minutes. During this time, in a medium pan sauté the chicken livers in clarified butter over a low heat setting until firm. Remove the livers using a slotted spoon onto a chopping board. Add the green onions, bell pepper, and pimento to the pan and sauté.

During this time, chop the livers fine and return them to the pan. Add the wild rice, mixing well. Add the minced garlic and parsley. Season the rice mixture to taste with salt and pepper.

When the birds are browned, remove from the oven and allow to cool enough to handle. Carefully stuff with rice mixture and place a slice of foie gras over each opening to cover the stuffing. Return stuffed birds to the oven for 10 minutes. Remove and garnish with chopped parsley. *Serves 2.*

Meats

FILET MIGNON DEMI-GLAS

Mignon, which means "small," is the cut of the steak used in this classic French preparation. The sauce *Demi-glas* is probably the most important of the French sauce bases, and is the root of literally thousands of brown sauces.

2 tbsp. clarified margarine	Pepper to taste
4 12-oz. beef tenderloin filets	1 cup Demi-glace Sauce
Salt to taste	1 tbsp. finely chopped parsley

In a large skillet or sauté pan, heat the clarified margarine on a medium setting. Season the filets with salt and pepper to your taste then sauté on each side for how done you prefer (about 6 minutes on each side for medium rare).

Place one in the center of each serving plate and top with an even covering of Demi-glace Sauce.

Garnish with a sprinkle of parsley. *Serves 4.*

GRILLED BEEF TENDERLOIN MEDALLIONS DRESSED

An early traveler to New Orleans commented in his journal that the people here eat more meat than any person of Europe could possibly imagine and that vegetables were reserved for the tables of the wealthy.

This same journalist was himself amazed that the children grew strong and healthy, in spite of their consumption of such great quantities of meat.

In this recipe, there are onions, tomatoes, and mushrooms to complement the tenderloin and balance the flavors.

3 12-oz. filets of beef tenderloin
Black peppercorns, fresh and
   cracked
2 large white onions

3 large tomatoes
12 large mushrooms
3 tbsp. Parmesan cheese
3 sprigs parsley, finely
   chopped, for garnish

Halve each filet "butterfly" style (you may have this done by
your butcher), separate, and season with black peppercorns.
   Cut each onion into three ½-inch slices, keeping the rings intact.
   Cut two ½-inch slices from each tomato, using the center cuts for
large slices.
   Place the filets on the grill on a medium heat setting along with
the onion, tomato slices, and mushrooms. Grilling about 3 minutes
on each side will render them medium-rare. The turning time is the
same for the onion and tomato slices.
   Alternately arrange the onion and tomato slices atop each
medallion. Sprinkle Parmesan cheese over the tomato slices.
   Arrange one dressed medallion per each serving plate. Garnish
with two mushroom buttons and a sprinkle of fresh parsley.
Serves 6.

STEAK AU POIVRE

There is no spice in the world that is used more than black pepper. It can be found in virtually every cuisine in the world, on
every table in the world. This classic dish should be made with
freshly cracked peppercorns to catch the fleeting spice perfume of
the peppercorn, which dissipates soon after the cracked pieces are
exposed to the air.
   Although precracked peppercorns—those that can be store-
bought from the spice shelf—are suitable, only the freshly cracked
will yield the subtle flavor that makes this dish so very popular.

2 tbsp. freshly cracked black peppercorns	1 oz. Cognac
	3 tbsp. softened butter
4 12-oz. filets of tenderloin	2 tbsp. finely chopped green onions
2 tbsp. oil	
2 tbsp. clarified butter	½ cup beef stock or bouillon

Crack peppercorns with a pestle or the bottom of a serving spoon. Coat steaks with cracked pepper, cover with waxed paper, and allow to stand for 1 hour.

In a large, heavy skillet, sauté the steaks in hot oil and butter over a moderate heat setting for about 4-5 minutes on each side for a medium-rare doneness. Remove steaks and hold in a warm place.

Pour off excess grease from pan, then deglaze with Cognac, scraping the bottom of the skillet of coagulated juices. Add 1 tbsp. of the softened butter and the green onions. Slowly simmer for 2 minutes. Pour in the stock or bouillon.

Increase heat setting and boil down rapidly. Remove from heat setting and swirl in remaining softened butter, a small amount at a time. Blend well, top the steaks with the sauce, and serve. *Serves 4.*

GRILLADES AND GRITS

One of our most cherished breakfast dishes is Grillades and Grits. It not only serves as a most traditional breakfast fare, but can also be found on the brunch, lunch, and late-night supper table.

2 tbsp. shortening	chopped
1 lb. veal scallops (⅛-inch thick)	1 tsp. tomato paste
	3 cloves minced garlic
1 small yellow onion, finely chopped	Salt to taste
	White pepper to taste
1 rib celery, finely chopped	⅛ tsp. thyme
½ green bell pepper, chopped	1 tsp. parsley, finely chopped
1 tbsp. flour	2 bay leaves
2 cups beef stock	1 cup white wine
2 tomatoes, seeded, peeled, and	3 cups grits, cooked

In a skillet, heat the shortening over medium heat. Brown the veal on both sides lightly. Remove from the skillet and set aside. Add the onion, celery, and green bell pepper to the fat in the skillet to sauté until tender (about 2 minutes). Add the flour, stirring constantly until the mixture becomes a dark brown roux. While stirring, add the beef stock, tomatoes, and tomato paste. Add the garlic and season with salt, white pepper, thyme, parsley, and bay leaves.

Lower the heat and simmer partially covered for 10 minutes. Add the white wine and stir. Add the veal scallops and cook for another 30 minutes at a low simmer. If needed, adjust the thickness of the sauce with a small amount of water.

Serve over a bed of grits. *Serves 4-6.*

ROAST LEG OF LAMB WITH 40 CLOVES OF GARLIC

Leg of lamb is probably my favorite roast of meat in existence. When I entertain, I often serve it, enjoying it as much as my guests do.

The 40 cloves of garlic is a classic French preparation that cannot be denied its enduring popularity.

1 5-lb. leg of lamb	1 yellow onion, sliced
2 tbsp. olive oil	2 ribs celery, chopped
Salt to taste	1 head garlic, peeled
1 tbsp. cracked black pepper	1 cup water
1 tbsp. rosemary, finely chopped	2 oz. brandy
	40 cloves garlic

Preheat oven to 375 degrees. Trim lamb leg of excess fat and the silvery fel or filament.

Rub the leg with olive oil then season with salt, pepper, and rosemary. Add sliced onion, celery, and garlic to the bottom of the roasting pan, then add water. Insert the rack in the pan then place the lamb leg on the rack, outside part facing up. Place into the oven and cook for 1 hour and 40 minutes. For a good medium-rare doneness, 20 minutes per pound is an ample cooking time.

Remove the leg from the oven and transfer to a slotted cutting board or another pan to retrieve the juices. Allow to stand for 10-15 minutes before carving.

Pour off excess juices from roasting pan. Deglaze pan with brandy, then sear garlic cloves on the stove over a medium-high heat setting until brown. Serve with lamb as garnish. *Serves 8.*

GRILLED MARINATED LEG OF LAMB

Marinating the leg of lamb for two entire days may seem just a bit excessive, but it takes that amount of time to get the best flavors of the marinade to imbue itself into the meat.

After that is done, only grilling is required to result in a most delicious dish.

MARINADE

5 cups full-bodied red wine
1 cup red wine vinegar
1 tbsp. salt
1 tbsp. black peppercorns
½ cup olive oil
6 bay leaves
1 tsp. thyme

1 tsp. rosemary
4 cloves minced garlic
6 sprigs parsley, finely
  chopped
1 7-8 lb. leg of lamb, boned and
  rolled out flat

Mix all marinade ingredients together in a mixing bowl. Place lamb in a roaster or any container large enough to accommodate. Pour marinade over lamb. Turn and baste lamb with marinade 4-5 times a day for 2 days, refrigerated.

Drain on a rack then place on a grill or spit over medium heat for 15 minutes on each side. If on an outdoor grill, you then may want to close the lid and slow cook on each side for 20 minutes. *Serves 6.*

GRILLED SPLIT RACK OF LAMB DIJON

As you can tell, mustard is one of my favorite ingredients, from Creole to Dijon.

The Dijon is best here for its tart flavor that gives the lamb a "bite" to savor.

MARINADE

2 cups red wine
1 cup Dijon mustard
2 bay leaves

4 cloves garlic, minced
2 sprigs thyme, fresh

Prepare a marinade in a medium bowl by combining the red wine, Dijon mustard, bay leaves, garlic, and fresh thyme.

1 1½ lb. rack of lamb
Salt to taste
1 tsp. cracked black pepper

½ tsp. thyme, dried
Olive oil

Season the lamb rack with the salt, cracked black pepper, and dried thyme. Coat the lamb with olive oil and refrigerate in the marinade for 24 hours.

Remove and allow lamb to return to room temperature. Preheat the grill and allow lamb to cook covered, off center of heat source, for 45 minutes. Remove and let stand for 5 minutes before carving. *Serves 2.*

MIXED GRILL OF LAMB, PORK, AND CHICKEN BEARNAISE

It really is the Béarnaise Sauce that changes this mixed grill from the mundane to the exceptional. The sauce itself was created by the great French chef Collinet, who named it after the birthplace of his king—Béarn.

2 cups Béarnaise Sauce
1 lb. lamb loin
1 lb. pork loin
3 whole chicken breasts

Black pepper, coarsely ground
½ tsp. paprika
1 tsp. finely chopped parsley

Prepare Béarnaise Sauce and set aside.

Slice both the lamb and pork loins into ½-inch thick medallions. Half each chicken breast, then cut each half into 3 equal pieces. Season lamb, pork, and chicken pieces on both sides with black pepper and paprika.

On a medium heat setting, first grill the lamb and pork for 3 minutes, then turn and put on the chicken pieces, turning after 2 minutes. Cook for another couple of minutes then remove from the grill along with the lamb and pork.

Arrange equal portions on serving plates with 2 medallions of each and a sprinkle of parsley. Serve Béarnaise on the side. *Serves 8.*

CALF'S LIVER SAUTEED WITH CARAMELIZED ONIONS AND BACON

I don't think anyone would deny (even the not-liver lovers) that the flavors of liver, onions, and bacon are a superb combination. Even in the cooking, the smells are sublime.

1 medium yellow onion, chopped	8 slices liver
1 tbsp. clarified butter	2 cups flour
½ lb. bacon, cut into 1-inch cubes	Salt to taste
	Black pepper to taste
½ cup cooking oil	1 tbsp. finely chopped parsley

In a heavy skillet, sauté the chopped onion in butter over medium heat until golden brown, occasionally draining the excess butter and reducing the heat to achieve an amber or caramel color. Drain and set aside. In the same skillet, fry the bacon until golden brown. Transfer to paper towels to drain.

In a separate sauté pan, heat the cooking oil over medium heat. Mix the flour with the salt and pepper and dredge the liver slices in the seasoned flour, then place in the sauté pan. Cook for 3-4 minutes on each side.

Serve 2 pieces of liver to each of four serving plates, topping each portion with equal amounts of onions, bacon strips, and a garnish of parsley. *Serves 4.*

ROAST TENDERLOIN OF PORK WITH APPLE AND MANGO SALSA

This is another entry of mine in the contemporary vein. Pork has become so low-fat and flavorful, it really is a delicious meat that can be enjoyed often. And with this salsa as a garnish it is particularly delectable.

2 8-oz. pork tenderloins
1 tbsp. olive oil
2 cloves minced garlic
Salt to taste
¼ tsp. black pepper
¼ tsp. ground cumin

1 tbsp. softened butter
1 mango, peeled, pitted, and
    sliced
1 apple, peeled, cored, and
    sliced into 8 wedges
⅛ tsp. ground cinnamon

In a medium roasting pan, rub the tenderloins with oil and garlic. Season with salt, black pepper, and cumin. Cover and chill for 4 hours to marinate, turning occasionally.

Preheat the oven to 350 degrees. Place the pork tenderloins into the oven and allow to roast for 50 minutes, basting every 20 minutes.

In a saucepan, melt the butter then slowly sauté the mango and apple slices until tender. Add cinnamon and turn. Remove and keep warm.

Transfer the pork to a chopping board and slice into ½-inch medallions. Arrange onto serving plates in a fan, then spoon mango and apple salsa alongside. *Serves 4.*

ROAST PORK LOIN WITH MUSTARD CREAM SAUCE

Although popular medicine has attempted to make foods like pork an indiscretion, anyone who exercises regularly and keeps himself fit can enjoy such a thing on occasion without too much guilt.

It's the pan drippings that make the Mustard Cream Sauce special. Enjoy it.

1 4-lb. pork loin   Black pepper
2 tbsp. cooking oil

STOCK

1 onion, diced   1 turnip, chopped
2 green onions, finely chopped   2 cloves garlic, chopped
1 carrot, minced   2 cups water

Preheat oven to 325 degrees.

Rub pork loin with cooking oil and black pepper. Using a baking rack with a drip pan, put in the onion, green onion, carrot, turnip, and garlic. Add the water.

Set the pork loin atop the drip pan and place in the oven. Bake for 2 hours and 15 minutes, adding water to drip pan, if needed. Baste occasionally.

Remove loin from the oven and keep warm. Again baste the loin with the juices and remove the drippings from the pan. Strain the juices through a fine sieve and reserve for the Mustard Cream Sauce. Discard vegetables.

MUSTARD CREAM SAUCE

Pan drippings from the pork   4 tbsp. Dijon mustard
  loin   1 pt. whipping cream
2 tsp. lemon juice   3 sprigs parsley, finely
Pinch salt   chopped, for garnish
Pinch white pepper

In a saucepan, heat pork drippings over a low heat setting. Add the lemon juice, salt, pepper, and mustard. While stirring with a wire whisk, allow the mixture to come to a simmer. Gradually pour in the whipping cream, continually stirring until the sauce begins to thicken, approximately 2 minutes.

Slice the pork loin into ½-inch slices, about 3 per serving. Spoon on the Mustard Cream Sauce and garnish with fresh parsley. *Serves 6.*

STEWED RABBIT

In Louisiana it is not uncommon to have a friend or neighbor drop by the house on the way home from a hunt with a share of game to deliver as a gift of sorts. This particular recipe is a hearty winter dish that can be prepared with farmed rabbits as well as wild rabbits.

1 2-lb. rabbit
Salt to taste
½ tsp. white pepper
½ cup cooking oil
1 small yellow onion, finely
  chopped
1 large tomato, cubed
2 cloves minced garlic
1 bouquet garni (1 sprig thyme,
  parsley, and a bay leaf tied in
  a string)

1 cup red wine
½ cup finely chopped ham
1 cup diced carrots
1 cup sliced mushrooms
1 tbsp. flour
1 cup boiling water or Brown
  Stock
4 cups cooked rice
1 tbsp. chopped parsley

Rinse rabbit in cold water then cut into pieces at the joints. Season pieces with salt and pepper.

In an earthenware pot, heat the oil to about 300 degrees (or for 3-4 minutes) over medium-high heat. Do not allow the oil to scorch or smoke. Add the onions and sauté until slightly browned, stirring occasionally. Add the rabbit pieces and brown on all sides. Add tomato, garlic, a bouquet garni, and the red wine. Reduce heat to a medium-low heat setting and allow rabbit to simmer for 15 minutes, covered.

Add ham, carrots, and sliced mushrooms. Stir, cover, and simmer for 15 minutes more. Stir in the flour, then add boiling water or Brown Stock. Stir and simmer for 20 minutes over a low heat.

Serve over cooked rice and garnish with parsley. *Serves 4.*

SWEETBREADS CLEMENCEAU

Although not as popular in America now as they once were, sweetbreads continue to find an appreciative audience in Europe, where they are served up with great enthusiasm.

New Orleans, being the Paris of the Americas, was home to gourmets from all parts of the world who had a particular taste for dishes made from offals. The situation remains the same now. True New Orleans gourmets are apt to choose the sweetbread or the tripe over a chicken dish at any opportunity.

This is a variation of a preparation that I also have in this collection served with shrimp and chicken. Clemenceau works with most any of our more popular foods.

1 lb. sweetbreads
1 bowl of cold water (enough
   to cover sweetbreads to soak)
Enough water to cover
¼ tsp. salt
2 tbsp. lemon juice
1 bay leaf
2 Idaho potatoes (to prepare
   Potatoes Brabant)

4 tbsp. clarified butter
⅓ tsp. black pepper
Pinch cayenne pepper
2 cups sliced mushrooms
4 cloves garlic, minced
2 cups petit pois peas, drained

Rinse sweetbreads in cold water. Place in a bowl of water and soak for 1 hour. Gently remove the outer skin or filament surrounding them. Place the sweetbreads in a large saucepan and fill with enough water to cover. Add the salt, lemon juice, and bay leaf. Simmer for 20 minutes, then drain and plunge into cold water long enough to cool to handling temperature.

Prepare Potatoes Brabant and hold aside on paper towels. Slice the sweetbreads into ½-inch slices. Heat the clarified butter in 2 large sauté pans, arranging sweetbreads flatly. Sauté on each side for 5 minutes over a medium heat setting or until golden brown. Season with black and cayenne peppers.

Add mushrooms, garlic, and potatoes and continue to sauté for 8-10 minutes until the mushrooms are tender. Drain off excess butter, add peas, and blend the combination evenly. *Serves 4.*

PEPPERED SWEETBREADS PERNOD

Offals found an admiring audience in the Crescent City. During the early days of the colony, the skirmishes with near-starvation taught the populace the important lesson of using absolutely everything that was available. These products—sweetbreads, hearts, livers—were treated with as much reverence in the kitchen as were the beefsteak and the truffle.

This dish, one of my own, sports a flavor reminiscent of absinthe days here. the Pernod, a licorice-flavored liqueur substitute for the prohibited absinthe, imparts a delicacy and unusualness that piques the appetite as it intrigues the diner.

Again, simplicity is the key here. Each ingredient is primary to the final savory flavor of this dish.

2 lb. sweetbreads
Enough water to cover
1 tsp. salt
1 tsp. whole black peppercorns
1 lemon
2 bay leaves
1 tsp. crushed black pepper

½ cup flour
½ cup clarified butter
6 large fresh button
    mushrooms, sliced
2 tbsp. Pernod
1 tbsp. finely chopped parsley

Fill a pot with enough water so that the sweetbreads are submerged. Add the salt and the black peppercorns. Halve one lemon and add the two halves to the pot. Add the bay leaves, cover, and allow to boil for 30 minutes. Remove from the heat and drain the sweetbreads in a colander until they are cool. Separate the sweetbread sections and cut them into ½-inch slices. Season with crushed black pepper. Dredge the sweetbreads in the flour.

In a large sauté pan heat the clarified butter, add the peppered sweetbreads, and sauté for 5 minutes, turning every 2 minutes or so. Add the sliced mushrooms and continue to sauté until the mushrooms are tender.

Add the Pernod then agitate the pan causing it to flame, hence burning off the excess alcohol. Serve the sweetbreads with the pan liquids poured over them. Garnish with chopped parsley. *Serves 4.*

Note: Mind the Pernod while it is heating. It is quite flammable.

PANEED VEAL SAUTE

Such a simple and delicious dish. It was common fare on our family table growing up. It is the bread crumbs that give a lightness to the batter that cannot be gotten from flour batters.

8 4-oz. veal cutlets	⅛ tsp. white pepper
1 egg	1 cup flour
2 cups milk	1 cup fine French bread crumbs
Dash Tabasco sauce	¼ cup oil
Salt to taste	1 tbsp. finely chopped parsley

Gently flatten the cutlets with a meat mallet.

In a medium mixing bowl, add the egg, milk, Tabasco, salt, and white pepper to make a batter. Whisk until well blended. Lightly coat the cutlets with flour then dredge through the batter. Coat each side of the cutlets with bread crumbs.

In a large sauté pan heat the oil over a medium heat setting then fry the cutlets for 3 minutes on each side until golden brown. Transfer to a dry cloth to drain and then serve 2 cutlets per person on serving plates. Garnish with a sprinkle of parsley. *Serves 4.*

BABY VEAL SAUTE
WITH LEMON BUTTER SAUCE

There was a time in New Orleans when beef was so terribly expensive that seldom did a New Orleanian ever see a beefsteak, other than in one of the more expensive restaurants. The veal at that time was, of course, not the fine, white baby veal that is readily available today. It tended to lean more toward baby calf. How times have changed.

This preparation is a good complement to the meat, and it is universally enjoyed.

8 4-oz. baby veal cutlets	¼ cup clarified butter
Salt to taste	1 oz. brandy
Black pepper to taste	Juice of ½ lemon
1 cup flour	2 tbsp. softened butter

Season the veal cutlets with salt to suit your taste and with black pepper using a pepper mill. Lightly flour each cutlet on a baking sheet. Heat the clarified butter in a large sauté pan or skillet on a low heat setting. Sauté the cutlets until lightly browned on each side, or about 1½ minutes per side. Baby veal is very delicate and takes little time to cook.

Remove the cutlets from the pan, discard the juices in the pan. Place the cutlets in a warm holding place. Still using the same pan and heat setting, deglaze pan with 1 oz. brandy, scraping the bottom. Mind the flame from the brandy; it is very flammable.

All the alcohol should burn off very quickly. Add the lemon juice and mix well. Strain the juices through a fine sieve into a small saucepan. Discard the residue.

Arrange two cutlets on each serving plate then fold in the softened butter into the sauce and top the cutlets with an even portion of sauce. *Serves 4.*

BRAISED VEAL CHOPS WITH CARAMELIZED ONIONS AND BRUSSELS SPROUTS

Like so many simple dishes, it is the carmelized onions and the garnish of the Brussels sprouts that make it special. The red wine finish in the deglazing tops off the balance of flavors.

2 medium yellow onions, sliced	Pepper to taste
2 tbsp. softened butter	1 cup red wine
1 tbsp. oil	2 tbsp. finely chopped shallots
1 tbsp. clarified butter	2 cloves garlic, minced
4 10-oz. veal chops	2 dozen Brussels sprouts
Salt to taste	1 tsp. chopped parsley

Preheat oven to 350 degrees.

In a medium sauté pan, sauté the onions in the softened butter over a medium heat setting until they achieve a dark amber color. Remove from heat and keep warm.

In a large skillet, heat the oil and clarified butter and sear chops on both sides, 3-4 minutes on each side. Season with salt and pepper, then arrange chops in an earthenware pot.

Deglaze the skillet with red wine, add the shallots and garlic, and simmer for 1 minute.

Pour the pan juices over the chops in the casserole, add Brussels sprouts, then cover and braise in the oven for 15-20 minutes.

Arrange the chops on serving plates surrounded by Brussels sprouts, then swirl with caramelized onions. Garnish with parsley. *Serves 4.*

BRAISED VEAL SHANK PROVENCALE

One of the more delectable, although often forgotten, cuts of meat, of veal, is the shank. It is rich in texture and surprisingly tender for a joint cut, and yields the silken juices that so perfectly thicken a sauce.

Tomatoes, onions, and garlic are the base ingredients of many a dish from France's province of Provence. Here I join the ingredients to the veal shank to produce a delicious variation on the southern French tradition.

1 cup flour
4 veal shanks (hind shanks)
¼ cup olive oil
2 cups sliced onion
1 cup dry white wine
2 tomatoes, peeled, seeded and chopped
1½ cups Brown Stock or beef bouillon

1 tsp. sweet basil
1 bay leaf
4 cloves minced garlic
1 tbsp. finely chopped parsley
Salt to taste
¼ tbsp. black pepper
2 cups cooked rice

Dredge the veal shanks in flour and shake off excess. Add olive oil to an iron skillet and heat over a medium heat setting. Brown shanks on both sides and during this time, sauté the onions in an earthenware pot over medium heat until browned. Transfer the veal shanks to the pot with the onions.

Drain the veal pan of its oil and then deglaze it with white wine, scraping the bottom of the browning juices. Pour these juices into the veal and onions. Stir in the tomatoes, stock, sweet basil, bay leaf, garlic, and parsley. Season with salt and black pepper. Cover and simmer on a low heat setting for about an hour, stirring occasionally.

Serve each shank in a circle of cooked rice. Provide a cocktail fork for the removal of bone marrow. *Serves 4.*

FILETS OF VENISON FOIE GRAS WITH CITRON GARNISH

We are the "sportsman's paradise" in Louisiana and often, probably more than in other places, we have the opportunity to enjoy the delicacies of our woods—such as venison.

This marriage of venison and foie gras is traditional and delicious, and deservedly so. The slight "wild" flavor of venison goes well with the luscious flavor of foie gras.

The caramelized lemon is my own addition.

Zest of 1 lemon
2 tbsp. water
1 tbsp. sugar
5 tbsp. softened butter
4 6-oz. venison tenderloins

¼ cup dry vermouth
1 tbsp. parsley, finely chopped
1 oz. pâté de foie gras, sliced
   for 4

Peel the zest of a lemon then cut the zest into very fine slices. In a small saucepan, boil peels until limp. Remove and drain. Place peels back into saucepan then add water and sugar. Simmer until water has evaporated and peels are lightly caramelized. Hold aside.

In a medium skillet, melt 2 tbsp. of the softened butter over a medium-high heat. When the butter sizzles, place the filets into skillet and cook for 5 minutes on each side until brown. Remove and transfer filets to a warm plate. Pour off pan juices and deglaze skillet with dry vermouth. Reduce liquid to 1 tbsp. and remove the sauce from the heat. Swirl in remaining 3 tbsp. softened butter and parsley.

Arrange one filet to each serving plate then place one slice of pâté atop each. Top with sauce and a crown of lemon peels. *Serves 4.*

GRILLED MARINATED TENDERLOIN OF VENISON

Louisiana has always been a "sportsman's paradise." Even today that expression is the state's motto. Venison, ducks, rabbits, turkeys—all forms of wild game and fish have been a principal part of our larder.

This marinade of my own design essentially augments the fine wild flavor of venison, without causing it to lose its distinctive inherent flavors and qualities.

VENISON AND SEASONINGS

1 3-4 lb. tenderloin of venison	1 cup cooking oil
1 tsp. coarse ground black pepper	1 tbsp. dried ground thyme
	2 tbsp. Dijon mustard

In a shallow baking pan, place the tenderloin of venison and season with the coarse ground black pepper on all sides. Rub on the cooking oil. Sprinkle on the ground thyme and rub on the Dijon mustard.

MARINADE

2 cups dry red wine	1 large onion, thinly sliced
½ cup Worcestershire	Salt to taste
½ cup soy sauce	Pinch ground bay leaf
2 cloves garlic, minced	Pinch cayenne pepper
2 tbsp. minced parsley	2 cups Marchand de Vin Sauce

In a mixing bowl, combine all marinade ingredients. Mix well.

Pour the marinade into the baking pan. Allow to marinate for 4 hours, turning about every hour.

Preheat the grill to a medium-high heat setting. Remove the tenderloin from the baking pan and drain off the excess marinade. Place the tenderloin on the heated grill and cook for 5 minutes, then turn and cook for an additional 4 minutes. Ideally, this dish should be cooked medium-rare and these times of grilling will assure that the venison does not overcook and will remain tender.

Remove and slice the meat into ½-inch thick medallions. Arrange neatly on serving plates and nap with the Marchand de Vin Sauce. *Serves 4.*

Note: I recommend a freshly grilled vegetable—tomato, green peppers, or leeks—to accompany the venison along with the Marchand de Vin Sauce.

Venison is not always readily available. A tenderloin of beef, pork, or a leg of lamb works well in this preparation.

Desserts

BANANAS IN ORANGE BUTTER CREAM

It was more than a single time that the inhabitants of numerous Caribbean islands, mostly the French as well as the free people of color, were forced to flee their estates because of slave uprisings. Many of those survivors—I say survivors because the rebellions generally ended in death for many—arrived in New Orleans to begin new lives. It is through those emigrants that we were influenced by the cuisine of the Caribbean. This dish is one that very much reflects that influence.

4 ripe bananas
2 tbsp. softened butter
Juice of ½ orange
Zest of ½ orange, grated
Juice of ½ lemon

Zest of ½ lemon, grated
½ tsp. brown sugar
¼ cup orange liqueur
½ cup water
4 scoops vanilla ice cream

Peel bananas and slice lengthwise in half.

In a large saucepan, melt the butter and add the bananas, orange juice, orange rind, lemon juice, and lemon rind and slowly simmer over a medium heat setting for 2 minutes. Add brown sugar, orange liqueur, and water. Simmer for 5 minutes over a low heat setting.

Remove bananas, serving 2 slices (1 whole banana) per plate. Add one scoop of vanilla ice cream, then top with remaining sauce. *Serves 4.*

ORANGE BEIGNETS

Beignets are a famous part of New Orleans culinary tradition. Coffee and beignets!

A writer once said that if you leave New Orleans without powdered sugar on your shoes (from beignets) then you haven't been to New Orleans.

This recipe is a twist on the original.

⅔ cup plus 2 tbsp. flour
⅔ cup water
¾ tsp. baking powder
Generous pinch of salt
1½ tbsp. softened butter
½ tbsp. finely grated orange
   rind

1 egg
2 cups vegetable oil
1 tbsp. powdered sugar
1 tsp. powdered cinnamon

In a saucepan, combine the flour, water, baking powder, salt, butter, and grated orange rind. Stir ingredients over a medium heat setting until mixture is well blended. Continue cooking until it begins to bond well and achieves a coarse, gummy texture. Remove from heat.

Spoon mixture into a ball and place in a food processor. Add the egg and blend for 15 seconds. Remove mixture and place into a pastry bag with a diamond tip.

Heat vegetable oil to 360 degrees in a deep-welled skillet. Squeeze out portions of about 4 inches of beignet mix into hot oil. Fry on both sides until golden brown. Remove and place beignets on dry cloth.

Combine powdered sugar and powdered cinnamon, mix generously and sprinkle over beignets. Serve hot. *Serves 6-8.*

CAFE BRULOT

Inspired by Cafe Royale, for which a spoon of Cognac with a sugar cube is seated across the rim of the coffee cup and flamed before being stirred into rich, pure coffee, this recipe was devised in New Orleans to end the perfect dining experience.

1 orange	1 oz. brandy
12 cloves	1 oz. orange liqueur
6 cups brewed coffee, dark roast	Twists from 1 lemon
	3 cinnamon sticks

Using a paring knife, carefully carve the peel from an orange in a coil fashion. Stud the peel with cloves and put aside.

Brew 6 cups of coffee and keep hot.

In an 8-ounce glass, combine brandy and the orange liqueur. Place the glass in hot water to heat the mixture for about 2 minutes. Add the orange peel, cinnamon sticks, and the lemon twists to soak in the liquor. Pour the heated liquor into a brûlot bowl or a flat-bottomed, stainless steel bowl.

To flambé: This is mostly done in a darkened room for presentation. Apply a lit match to the side of the bowl to ignite the liquor. Stir using a ladle. Slowly pour in the coffee while stirring. When the flame is extinguished, this is the correct balance. Ladle small amounts of the strained liquid into demitasse cups. *Serves 6.*

BREAD PUDDING WITH BOURBON SAUCE

As in the kitchens of their French forefathers, the Creoles were a thrifty lot and never would have dreamed of losing the least amount of any food product to waste.

Even the unused "heel" of a French bread loaf, or stale bread, would be resurrected to a most delicious dessert in Bread Pudding. The fact is that the best bread puddings are made from stale bread, because only stale bread retains the lightness and buoyancy of texture once turned into the custard base.

The sauce can differ in as many ways as the garnish of the pudding itself. Rum or brandy make ready substitutions to the bourbon whiskey.

Nonstick vegetable spray	4 eggs
4 cups cubed French bread	1 ½ cups sugar
1 cup canned fruit cocktail	2 tbsp. vanilla
½ cup raisins	2 tbsp. clarified butter
1½ qt. milk	

Preheat oven to 350 degrees.

Lightly coat the bottom of a large baking dish with nonstick vegetable spray. Line the bottom with half of the breading. Cover with fruit cocktail and raisins. Top this with the remaining bread.

Heat the milk to a boil.

In a large mixing bowl, beat the eggs, sugar, and vanilla with a wire whisk. Add hot milk, mix well, then pour this mixture over the bread and fruit combination. Allow the bread to soak up the liquid.

Dot the surface of the bread pudding with clarified butter, then bake until firm, approximately 25 minutes.

Serve hot or cold, cut into squares, with the following sauce.

BOURBON SAUCE

2 cups hot milk	2 tbsp. soft butter
2 eggs	1 tbsp. vanilla
½ cup sugar	1 oz. bourbon whiskey
3 tbsp. corn starch	

Heat milk.

In a double boiler over a medium-low heat setting, mix eggs, sugar, corn starch, and butter. Gradually stir in the hot milk using a wire whisk, and stir constantly until the sauce thickens. Stir in the vanilla and bourbon and serve by pouring over the bread pudding. *Serves 6-8.*

PRALINE CHEESECAKE

Pralines have always been considered *the* Creole delicacy and are associated with the Creole women who made them—*pralinieres*, as they were called. These delicate but very sweet candies come in many variations. I most prefer the pecan version. I demonstrate their use in a sauce that complements my favorite dessert, cheesecake.

CHEESECAKE CRUST

¾ cup graham cracker crumbs   1 tsp. brown sugar
½ tbsp. sugar   1 tbsp. softened butter

Preheat oven to 375 degrees.

In a medium mixing bowl, combine graham cracker crumbs, sugar, brown sugar, and butter and mix well. Spread evenly over the bottom of a 9-inch springform pan while pressing lightly. Refrigerate crust while preparing filling.

FILLING

3 pkg. (8-oz. size) cream cheese,   1 cup sugar
   room temperature   1 tbsp. praline liqueur
4 eggs   1 tbsp. lemon juice
1 tsp. vanilla extract

In a large mixing bowl, beat the cream cheese, using an electric mixer, until light. Add the eggs, vanilla, sugar, praline liqueur, and lemon juice and continue beating until creamy and light.

Pour the filling into the crust and bake for 35 minutes. During this time, prepare the topping.

TOPPING

2 cups sour cream   5 pecans, shelled and halved,
1 tbsp. sugar   for garnish
1 tsp. vanilla extract

In a medium mixing bowl, using a wooden spoon, cream together the sour cream, sugar, and vanilla extract.

When the cheesecake is done baking, remove from the oven and spread the topping evenly over the surface. Bake for 5 more minutes.

Cool the cheesecake in the pan on a wire rack. Refrigerate for 4 hours or overnight. Remove the side of springform pan. Cut cheesecake into wedges. Garnish each wedge with a pecan half. *Serves 8-10.*

CHERRIES JUBILEE

This dessert derives from an ancient recipe of Bourgogne, the Burgundy province of France, which is made there with a brandy called "marc," the distilled liquor of red Burgundy wine.

In this version we see the inevitable "American" influence on this Creole presentation with the use of bourbon whiskey.

1 oz. Wild Turkey bourbon whiskey	4 oz. cherry juice, reserved from canned cherries
1 oz. cherry brandy	2 tbsp. sugar
36 dark sweet, pitted, canned cherries	2 pt. vanilla ice cream

In a small rock glass combine the Wild Turkey and the cherry brandy. Heat the liquor "double boiler" fashion using a small pot filled with enough water so that the glass will sit in one inch of water. Heat over a low heat setting and allow water to simmer. Liquor may remain at that temperature until ready to serve.

In a separate saucepan, heat the cherries in their own juice on a low heat setting. Add the sugar and stir until dissolved. Allow mixture to simmer for 5 minutes.

Spoon out one generous scoop of ice cream into each of six small bowls. To flame the cherry sauce, pour the heated liquor into a ladle and carefully ignite it over the sauce. Slowly stir using the ladle until the alcohol burns out and the flame is extinguished.

Spoon an equal portion of cherries (6 per serving) and sauce over ice cream. *Serves 6.*

Note: Use extreme care when handling the liquor—it is extremely flammable.

COUPE DUCHESSE

Our culinary efforts are sometimes a bit filling, this is why such desserts as this are a delight to conclude an evening of dining.

1 peach, skinned, pitted, and diced
1 pear, skinned, seeded, and diced
1 cup seedless green grapes

8 red cocktail cherries, halves
½ cup Cointreau liqueur
4 scoops French vanilla custard ice cream

In a small mixing bowl, combine the fruits with the Cointreau. Cover and chill in the refrigerator for one hour.

Spoon two generous scoops of ice cream into each of four chilled glass dessert dishes and top with the macerated fruit mixture. Serve immediately. *Serves 4.*

COUPE PRINCESSE

Similar to the classic Pêche Melba, this dessert employs port wine instead of grenadine syrup to give it a more interesting flavor.

2 generous scoops French vanilla custard ice cream
1 fresh peach, skinned, halved, and pitted

2 tbsp. red currant jelly
2 tbsp. roasted, sliced almond slivers
2 tbsp. port wine

In two glass dessert dishes, place the ice-cream scoops, the peach halves, and top with the currant jelly, roasted almond slivers, and the port wine. Serve immediately. *Serves 2.*

LEMON CREPES

This is merely a delicious departure from the usual crêpe recipe. But, it is a good enough deviation that they can be enjoyed as a dessert with nothing more than a little dusting of powdered sugar to finish off the sweetness.

Zest and juice of 1 lemon
2 cups milk
3 eggs
2 cups flour

2 tbsp. clarified butter
Nonstick vegetable spray or oil
Powdered sugar or Lemon
    Creme Filling

Grate the zest of one lemon. Squeeze the juice from the lemon through a cloth or fine sieve. In a saucepan, add the grated rind and lemon juice to the milk. Bring to a boil then allow to cool. Add the eggs and beat mixture using a wire wisk. Add the flour and clarified butter. Whisk and pass through a fine sieve. Allow to stand for a few minutes.

Coat a crêpe pan with vegetable spray or oil. Heat pan over a medium-low heat setting. Pour enough batter to thinly coat the pan. When the crêpes begin to separate around the edges, turn using a crêpe spatula.

Lemon crêpes may be served immediately hot and dusted with powdered sugar, or refrigerated and served cold with Lemon Cream Filling. *Makes 12 crêpes.*

LEMON CREAM CREPES

Using the Lemon Crêpe recipe with the addition of this cream filling makes a wonderful dessert. Because everything can be made ahead of time, it makes a nice end to a meal where the host can relax and enjoy dessert with his guests.

FILLING

2 lemons	4 eggs
¼ cup softened butter	12 Lemon Crêpes
1 cup powdered sugar	

Grate the rind of one of the lemons. Squeeze the juice from both lemons then strain through a fine sieve. Using a double boiler, melt the butter over a medium heat setting. Add sugar, lemon juice, and grated rind and mix well. Beat eggs using a wire whisk then pour into butter mixture. Continually whisk until mixture thickens and becomes smooth and creamy. Pour filling into a bowl and place immediately over a larger bowl of ice to cool, stirring occasionally. Refrigerate for 45 minutes before use.

Prepare 12 Lemon Crêpes.

Using a piping bag or spoon, pipe equal portions of filling into each crêpe, roll them up and serve 2 crêpes per serving. *Serves 6.*

CREPES MAISON

As simple as this recipe is, it is one that has delighted many a guest at Galatoire's. It is particularly popular with the regular local customers who have reserved little room for dessert, yet want something light and sweet to complete their meal.

CREPE BATTER

¾ cup flour	3 eggs
2 tsp. sugar	¾ cup milk
½ tsp. salt	1 tbsp. butter, minced

To make the crêpes, sift the flour, sugar, and salt together in a bowl. In a small mixing bowl, beat the eggs. Add the milk, then the dry ingredients, and beat the batter in a mixer on medium speed or blend in a blender until the batter is smooth. Allow the batter to sit for about 1 hour before cooking.

Heat a 6-inch crêpe pan over medium-high heat. Lift the pan from the heat, and, using a pastry brush, brush the bottom of the pan lightly with a little melted butter. Premeasure 2 tbsp. of batter, and pour the batter into the middle of the pan. Quickly tilt the pan so that the batter spreads evenly over the bottom. Return the pan to the heat, and brown the crêpe lightly. Turn the crêpe with a spatula, and brown the other side. Repeat the above process until all the batter is used, brushing the pan with melted butter as needed. Place the crêpes (there will be 12-16 of them) between layers of wax paper until they are ready to fill.

FILLING

12 tbsp. (6 oz.) currant jelly	**¼ cup Triple Sec liqueur**
½ cup sliced almonds	**3 tbsp. sifted powdered sugar**

Spread 1 tbsp. of jelly on each crêpe. Fold the crêpes into thirds. Place them side by side in an oblong baking pan. Sprinkle the crêpes with sliced almonds. Place the crêpes under the broiler for 3-5 minutes or until the almonds are lightly toasted. Remove the crêpes from the heat, and sprinkle Triple Sec liqueur and powdered sugar over them.

Allow 2 crêpes per serving. *Serves 6-8.*

CREPES SUZETTE

Mademoiselle Suzette is said to have been an actress, and member of the Comédie-Française in 1837. It was in a play that this dish was served on the stage and was named by its creator after the beguiling actress.

12 Crêpes (see Crêpes Maison)	**2 oranges, peels only**
¼ cup softened butter	**1 lemon, peel only**
¼ cup sugar	**½ oz. Grand Marnier liqueur**
1 orange, juiced	**½ oz. Cointreau liqueur**
1 lemon, juiced	**½ oz. brandy**

Prepare Crêpes and set aside momentarily.

In a large saucepan, melt the softened butter over a low heat setting. Add the sugar and mix well. Add the orange and lemon juices and the orange and lemon peels. Simmer slowly until peels are transluscent. Fold each crêpe in half, then into quarters and place into saucepan.

Pour in Grand Marnier, Cointreau, and brandy. Tip the saucepan slightly and ignite. Agitate the pan until the flame is exhausted. Carefully remove the crêpes and place three to a serving plate. Top with remaining sauce. *Serves 4.*

CARAMEL CUP CUSTARD

The smooth richness of this dessert is achieved by never allowing the custard to simmer during its cooking. In which case, it will remain velvety smooth in texture, while the caramel gives it a depth of flavor that enhances the total effect.

CARAMEL

1 cup sugar	**Water**
1½ tbsp. water	

Preheat oven to 350 degrees.

To make the caramel, place the sugar and water into a small, thick saucepan over a medium-low heat setting. Heat while constantly stirring with a wooden spoon until mixture turns a pale, dark caramel color. Arrange 12 custard cups in a baking pan or bain-marie. Fill the bottom of the pan with an inch of water. Pour enough caramel into the custard cups to cover the bottoms.

CUSTARD

1 qt. milk	**½ tsp. vanilla extract**
4 eggs	**Pinch nutmeg**
¾ cup sugar	

Prepare the custard by heating milk in a medium pot over a medium heat setting until just under a boil. In a large, stainless steel mixing bowl, beat the eggs, adding sugar, vanilla extract, and nutmeg until well blended. Remove milk from heat, then pour into egg mixture whisking vigorously until sugar has dissolved. Pour custard mixture, through a fine sieve, back into pot. Fill each custard cup with the mixture then slide into oven to bake for 45-55 minutes until cooked through. Test for doneness with a toothpick. Remove from the oven and allow to cool. Transfer to refrigerator for 2 hours.

To serve, press the outer surface of the custard around the rim, then turn out into a small dish. *Serves 12.*

Note: For a richer flavor, add a bit of amaretto to the custard mixture before filling the custard cups.

CUSTARD ICE CREAM WITH CHOCOLATE CREME DE MENTHE SAUCE AND SLIVERED ALMONDS

Again the simplicity of this dessert complements the close of a grand meal. Something sweet and light is just the right thing for our New Orleans climate and this fits the bill.

½ cup chocolate sauce
2 tbsp. crème de menthe
   liqueur
4 scoops French vanilla custard
   ice cream

2 tbsp. roasted slivered
   almonds
2 sprigs fresh mint

In a small saucepan, heat the chocolate over a low heat setting. Add the crème de menthe liqueur and stir until well blended. Hold aside warm.

In 2 glass dessert dishes, spoon 2 scoops each of French vanilla custard ice cream. Spoon over the heated chocolate mint sauce and sprinkle with the slivered almonds. Garnish each with a sprig of fresh mint. *Serves 2.*

MANCHAC MOCHA MOUSSE

Manchac is a small neighboring city that practically exists on water. It was once a place for pirates, and many ships that could not come into port in New Orleans would moor there while doing the commerce of selling whatever the goods they carried.

Even today there exists a number of excellent family-style seafood restaurants there.

½ cup milk	2 egg yolks
2 tsp. instant espresso powder	2 tbsp. sugar
1 oz. semisweet chocolate, chopped, plus additional shavings for garnish	1 tbsp. unsalted butter
	1 large egg white
	2 tbsp. powdered sugar

In a small saucepan, combine milk, espresso powder, and chopped chocolate. Heat mixture over medium heat setting, continuously stirring until chocolate is hot and melted.

In a medium, stainless steel bowl, whisk together the egg yolks and sugar. Slowly add to the chocolate mixture, whisking constantly.

Return the saucepan to the stove, add butter, and cook over a medium-low heat, stirring constantly until sauce thickens. Do not allow sauce to scorch or boil. Transfer mixture to another bowl. Place this bowl in a larger bowl of crushed ice and water and stir until the mixture cools.

In a small bowl, beat the egg white until foamy. Add the powdered sugar while beating continuously until it forms stiff peaks. Fold the egg white into the chocolate mixture gently until well blended. Cover and chill for 1 hour.

Spoon the mousse into 2 champagne glasses and garnish with chocolate shavings. *Serves 2.*

MANGO SORBET
WITH MELON COMPOTE

This cold dessert is as refreshing as anything can be. Make enough, you'll want more.

4 mangos, peeled, pitted, and cut into large pieces
1 cup Sauterne wine
¾ cup sugar
¼ cup apricot brandy
¼ cup water
1 cup mango, peeled, pitted, and cubed into ¼-inch pieces
1 cup honeydew melon, peeled, seeded, and cubed into ¼-inch pieces
1 cup cantalope, peeled, seeded, and cubed into ¼-inch pieces
6 mint leaves, for garnish

Puree the 4 mangoes in blender. Add Sauterne wine and ½ cup of the sugar and blend until sugar dissolves. Transfer mixture to ice-cream maker; process according to manufacturer's directions to operate. Freeze covered.

In a small, heavy skillet, combine the apricot brandy, water, and the remaining ¼ cup of sugar. Stir over medium heat until the sugar dissolves. Allow to simmer about 3-4 minutes. Remove and chill unitil cold. Gently fold mango, honeydew, and cantalope melon cubes into syrup.

Scoop sorbet into dessert glasses (2 small scoops per glass) then top with the melon compote. Garnish with a mint leaf. *Serves 6.*

CHOCOLATE PATE AMANDINE
WITH STRAWBERRY CREAM

This is a dessert for serious chocolate lovers. The combination of the flavors of Cointreau liqueur, almonds, and strawberries makes it a contemporary classic.

18 oz. baking chocolate
2⅓ cup softened butter
3 cups unsweetened cocoa
  powder
1 cup sugar
½ cup water

6 egg yolks
3 eggs
¼ cup Cointreau or Grand
  Marinier liqueur
2 tbsp. vanilla
1½ cups sliced roasted almonds

Line an 8-cup rectangular mold with freezer paper. In a double boiler, combine the chocolate and the butter with the cocoa. Melt slowly over boiling water, stirring with a wooden spoon until smooth. Transfer to a large bowl.

Cook sugar and water in a small saucepan over a low heat setting, stirring until sugar dissolves. Increase heat and simmer for 3 minutes. In a medium bowl, whisk the egg yolks, eggs, Cointreau, and vanilla.

Stir the syrup into the chocolate mixture. Fold in 1 cup of the sliced almonds, reserving ½ cup for garnish. Whisk in the egg mixture. Pour into the prepared mold and cover with plastic wrap. Refrigerate overnight.

STRAWBERRY CREAM

1 pt. fresh strawberries
4 tbsp. sugar

2 pt. heavy cream

Rinse the strawberries in cold water. Halve 6 strawberries and reserve for garnish. Hull and halve the remaining strawberries. Put them in a blender of food processor, adding the sugar and heavy cream, and blend until very smooth. Refrigerate until ready to use.

Cut the chocolate pâté into thin slices. Spoon the Strawberry Cream onto serving plates. Set the pâté slices atop the cream. Garnish with a sprinkle of sliced almonds and a strawberry half. *Serves 12.*

BOOLIE'S PRALINES

My maternal grandmother, Boolie Evans, was the family expert at several true Creole delicacies. Pralines was one of her best offerings.

This recipe duplicates hers, the resulting confection a reminder of sweeter times.

1 12-oz. can evaporated milk	**5 cups pecans**
½ cup butter	**Pinch salt**
3 cups sugar	**2 tsp. vanilla**
3 cups brown sugar	

Combine all the above ingredients into a medium, heavy-bottomed pot. Melt over a medium-low heat setting while stirring until mixture thickens and achieves the soft-ball stage, where it forms a ball when dropped in cold water. Remove from fire and allow to cool for 5 minutes while stirring.

Ladle cookie-sized portions onto a marble top or wax paper. Allow to cool completely. *Makes 2 dozen.*

RUM PRALINES

With many of the native Caribbeans who came to New Orleans to escape slave uprisings on their own islands came the products that they were accustomed to having on hand and enjoying. Rum was a principal item and was a staple of the New Orleans Cafe society, along with Cognac, long before the liquors of Scotland and Tennessee—scotch and bourbon—were even available. It was as natural as adding sugar to coffee when rum became an ingredient in the popular local confection called pralines.

2 cups white sugar
¾ cup brown sugar
½ cup butter
1 cup milk

2 cups pecan pieces
2 tsp. vanilla extract
1 oz. dark rum

In a large saucepan, combine sugar, brown sugar, butter, milk, pecans, vanilla extract, and dark rum. Cook slowly over a medium heat setting for 20 minutes. Stir until the soft-ball stage, when small amounts can form balls when dropped in cold water.

Spoon small portions (about 1 tbsp.) onto wax paper in cookie form and allow to cool for 20-30 minutes before removing from wax paper. *Makes approximately 2½ dozen pralines.*

HOT CHOCOLATE ALMOND SUNDAE WITH CREME DE MENTHE SAUCE

Again the simplicity of this dessert complements the close of a grand meal. Something sweet and light is just the right thing for our New Orleans climate and this fits the bill.

½ cup chocolate sauce
2 tbsp. crème de menthe
  liqueur
4 scoops French vanilla custard
  ice cream

2 tbsp. roasted, slivered
  almonds
2 sprigs fresh mint

In a small saucepan, heat the chocolate over a low heat setting. Add the crème de menthe liqueur and stir until well blended. Hold aside warm.

Into 2 glass dessert dishes, spoon 2 scoops each of the French vanilla custard ice cream. Spoon over the heated chocolate mint sauce and sprinkle with the slivered almonds. Garnish each with a sprig of fresh mint. *Serves 2.*

Index